Defending the South

Defending the South

Our Homes, Our Way of Life,
and Our Sacred Honor

FERDINAND CARSON

DEFENDING THE SOUTH
OUR HOMES, OUR WAY OF LIFE, AND OUR SACRED HONOR

iUniverse books may be ordered through booksellers or by contacting:

iUniverse
1663 Liberty Drive
Bloomington, IN 47403
www.iuniverse.com
1-800-Authors (1-800-288-4677)

Because of the dynamic nature of the Internet, any web addresses or links contained in this book may have changed since publication and may no longer be valid. The views expressed in this work are solely those of the author and do not necessarily reflect the views of the publisher, and the publisher hereby disclaims any responsibility for them.

Any people depicted in stock imagery provided by Thinkstock are models, and such images are being used for illustrative purposes only. Certain stock imagery © Thinkstock.

ISBN: 978-1-4917-9071-7 (sc)
ISBN: 978-1-4917-9068-7 (e)

Library of Congress Control Number: 2016905447

Print information available on the last page.

iUniverse rev. date: 4/7/2016

To Vivien

You people of the South don't know what you are doing. This country will be drenched in blood, and God only knows how it will end. It is all folly, madness, a crime against civilization! You people speak so lightly of war; you don't know what you're talking about. War is a terrible thing! You mistake, too, the people of the North. They are a peaceable people but an earnest people, and they will fight, too. They are not going to let this country be destroyed without a mighty effort to save it... Besides, where are your men and appliances of war to contend against them? The North can make a steam engine, locomotive, or railway car; hardly a yard of cloth or pair of shoes can you make. You are rushing into war with one of the most powerful, ingeniously mechanical, and determined people on Earth—right at your doors. You are bound to fail. Only in your spirit and determination are you prepared for war. In all else you are totally unprepared, with a bad cause to start with. At first you will make headway, but as your limited resources begin to fail, shut out from the markets of Europe as you will be, your cause will begin to wane. If your people will but stop and think, they must see in the end that you will surely fail.

William Tecumseh Sherman
Upon hearing of the secession of South Carolina
1860

Contents

Preface

Over the years I have collected a large amount of historical information about my Carson family. Now I think it's time to publish some of this information so that others may have an accurate picture of life on a Southern plantation and the relationship between black and white people around the time of the War Between the States.

In 1954 when I was a teenager, my family moved to Reynolds, Georgia, where my father took up farming and farmed much of the same land that his ancestors once farmed. I completed high school at Reynolds. After I graduated from Georgia Tech in 1960, my wife and I went to Illinois for two years. We returned to Reynolds in 1962 and lived there until 1965. During those years, we were frequent visitors to the original Carson plantation house. For a period of six months in 1962 we actually lived in another house on the original Carson land. Since then we have continued to visit the area from time to time.

Much of what I have written is from my own personal experience and knowledge of my family. More is about the area around Reynolds and northern Macon County, Georgia, and some is from stories handed down to me by my father. In addition I have consulted many documents from my personal collection including: newspaper clippings from the 1860's and later, unpublished manuscripts about family members, notes from the family Bible, tombstone inscriptions, courthouse records such as old deeds and marriage licenses, and personal letters. I've also had many conversations with old-timers from the area. There's a bibliography at the end of the book citing additional sources.

Events which did not actually happen to my family are typical of things that really did happen to other families in the area at the time, or might have happened given the mind-set of Southerners at the time. Most of the characters in this story, including most of the slaves, were real people with their real names. I've tried to give an accurate picture of life on a Southern plantation to the best of my understanding.

This is my second book. The first was *Beginning at a Stone*, a history of Muirs Chapel United Methodist Church in Greensboro, North Carolina.

Acknowledgements

Thanks to Tony Croce for checking the accuracy of the information about the battles mentioned in this book.

Thanks to Martha Decker for her editorial expertise and comments.

Special thanks to Catherine Foster for line editing this book.

Introduction

Defending the South is based on the true story of Joe Carson, a signer of Georgia's Ordinance of Secession, and his four sons who volunteered to defend the South against Northern aggression. The book describes everyday life on the Carson Plantation before, during, and after the War Between the States. It examines Southern attitudes about the war and - from a Southern viewpoint - the causes and after-effects of the war.

Note that I use the term "War Between the States" rather than the more common term, "Civil War." That's because a civil war is a war within one country and I believe the War Between the States was a war between two separate nations: the United States and the Confederate States of America. Many Southerners will recognize the terms "The Late Unpleasantries" and "The War of Northern Aggression" -- anything but the "Civil War." That's a Yankee term.

Chapter 1

John Thomas Begins the Story

Our inn was in Knoxville, Georgia, on the Federal Road that led from Macon, Georgia, to Montgomery, Alabama. Beyond Macon, the road went north to Washington, DC by way of Augusta, and southwest of Montgomery you could follow the Federal Road all the way to New Orleans. It was a busy highway serving travelers from all over the United States and sometimes even an occasional foreigner. Most of the travelers stopped to refresh themselves at our inn. Among them were touring theatrical companies, freight wagons, homesteaders seeking new lives in the West, Henry Clay, James Polk, Aaron Burr under arrest, evangelists, and traders. Even the Marquis de Lafayette and his entourage visited our inn.

The United States Government began to establish the Federal Road in 1805 when the Creek Indians reluctantly gave permission for the United States Government to open a horse path through their territory to facilitate mail service between Washington and New Orleans. In 1811, the road was improved so that it could be used as a military road because war with England was looming on the horizon. More improvements were made in 1819 so that the road was suitable for stage coaches. The government spared no expense for this latter improvement. The road was widened to twenty feet and tree stumps were cut down to a height of six inches or less. Maintenance costs were high because rain frequently washed gullies in the road and sometimes washed bridges away.

In 1848, the first telegraph line from Washington to New Orleans was built along the road and the Federal Road then became known as the Wire Road. Along much of the route, the wires were simply nailed to trees.

The Federal Road crossed the Flint River several miles south of Knoxville on a covered bridge. Indian Agent Benjamin Hawkins (appointed by George Washington) once had a plantation there with large herds of cattle and hogs. Hawkins didn't want his livestock to wander away and he didn't want to be accused of stealing the Indians' animals so the bridge had a gate at each end to prevent the animals from crossing the river. I think my Pa was a friend of Mr. Hawkins.

The Flint River arises just south of Atlanta and flows generally southward to its confluence with the Chattahoochee River. From there, the combined rivers are called the Apalachicola and flow across the panhandle of Florida into the Gulf of Mexico. The Indians called the Flint River "Thronateeska," which roughly translated means "place for picking up flint stones."

When I was born, the Flint River was the boundary between Georgia and the Creek Indian Territory. I can remember seeing Indian children playing on the far shore when I was a child, but most of the twenty thousand Creeks left Georgia for Oklahoma when I was about ten years old. White people rushed in to settle the former Indian Territory and establish plantations. Andrew Jackson was president at that time. The expression, "If the Good Lord's willin' and the Creeks don't rise," refers to the Creek Indians, not to bodies of water, because a Creek uprising was a real threat for settlers on the frontier of Georgia before the Indians left.

Our inn was across the road from the courthouse, so in addition to travelers we had many customers who came to town on court business. We also had a contract with the county to provide meals for the jurors. Stagecoaches got fresh horses at our stable, too. Our hands changed the horses quickly and efficiently while the driver and his passengers ate. Altogether, the inn was very busy and very profitable.

There were nine of us children, not counting Cadwell who died when he was just three.

I remember the first time we took our sister Annie along with us to pick those bronze-colored wild grapes called scuppernongs. She was about eight years old. It was in late September, a perfect early Autumn day, and we found the scuppernongs growing in the woods just a short distance from the inn. We immediately set to work, picking as fast as we could and eating as many as we picked. I noticed that Annie was not picking nor eating. She said, "I don't like scuppernongs. I want to go home."

I said, "Why? Why don't you like them? Are they too sour?"

"No," she said, "They're too tough and they've got seeds in them."

I said, "Silly, don't eat the hulls. Squeeze them like this, see. The insides pop out and you can eat them. Spit the seeds out, but save the hulls in your bucket."

She looked at me with curiosity and asked, "Why do we save the hulls?"

"You'll see," I said with a wink. After that she picked and ate as many as the rest of us.

We picked and ate and ate and picked until our buckets and our bellies were full, and we gave the hulls to Aunt Bessie when we got home. When I handed her the buckets, she said, "Oh Lawdy, Master John, you done brought a passel of scuppernongs! They'll make a mess of fine pies!"

Cooking seemed to come naturally to Aunt Bessie. She kept our new cast iron cook stove -- the latest design -- hot all the time because she never knew when she might need to prepare a meal on short notice. Daniel and Nelson fetched water and kept her supplied with firewood.

Annie said, "Can I watch?"

"Why sho, honey chile," said Aunt Bessie. "Hand me four of them pie tins there under the sink and then set yo'self right over there."

Aunt Bessie boiled our hulls to soften them along with a few scuppernongs that we hadn't eaten, and then mashed them. She mixed in sugar, flour, and a little water and poured this mixture into the pie tins. She rolled out a little biscuit dough, cut it into strips, and laid it over the top. Then she baked this until it was done. The aroma of the pies filled the inn, and when the pies came out of the oven and had time to cool, the result was a sort of cobbler. We scooped it out of the pie tins into bowls with a large spoon, and oh my, that was fine eating. We told Ma and Pa they couldn't have any because they hadn't picked any scuppernongs. But, of course, we knew that Ma and Pa had to stay and run the inn and couldn't go along, so we relented and gave some to them and the whole family. Aunt Bessie got some, too.

Once, I asked Aunt Bessie how old she was. She replied, "Law', chile, I don't know how old I is, but if you 'member the night yo' granma got married, that's the night I was born."

One day a train of wagons loaded with men stopped at our inn. We learned that Mr. William Ward had recruited them from Milledgeville and Macon, and they were on their way to help the people of Texas in their struggle for independence from Mexico.

Eighteen-year-old Joanna Troutman lived near our inn. After Aunt Bessie had fed the men and Nelson and Daniel had fed and watered the mules, the men were preparing to depart. Miss Troutman approached Mr. Ward and said, "Sir, we heard you might be coming, so I made this flag for you. See, it's a big blue star on a nice piece of white silk. On the back I sewed two inscriptions, one which reads, 'Liberty or Death,' and another inscription in Latin that I found in a book. Maybe it will bring you luck."

Mr. Ward accepted the flag and said, "Why, thank you, Miss. We'll fly it proudly when we get into a battle, and those Mexicans will know who they're tangling with."

We heard later that Mr. Ward and fifty-five members of his "Georgia Battalion" had been executed at Goliad, Texas, but the Lone Star of their battle-tattered flag had become the official emblem of Texas.

Another of my boyhood memories was of Uncle Lucas. Uncle Lucas was too old and feeble to do much work, so all he did was sit on our porch and listen for the stage coach. When he heard the stage coach driver announcing his imminent arrival by blowing his trumpet, Uncle Lucas would hurry to the kitchen and alert Aunt Bessie, who quickly set a meal on the table for the hungry travelers.

Many were the evenings when we children sat at Uncle Lucas' feet and listened to his stories. He was a better storyteller than either Ma or Pa.

I remember when he died. Although Uncle Lucas was not a member of our church, Aunt Bessie wanted him to have a church funeral. We all went and we gave all the slaves the day off so they could go, too. We were surprised to see how the slaves celebrated. They said Uncle Lucas had gone home to be with Jesus.

We noticed that Nelson brought Uncle Lucas' favorite tin cup to the funeral, and placed it on the grave at the end of the service. The cup was useless because Nelson had punched several holes in it. We asked Nelson what that was all about. He said, "Haints needs things same as people. We gives them things so they rest and don't wander. The holes makes it useless so ain't nobody gwine to steal it."

As soon as the funeral ceremony was over, Ma, Pa, my sister Emily Jane, and I hurried back to the inn so we could be there when the next stage arrived. Ma and Emily Jane worked in the kitchen in Aunt Bessie's place that day. Two of our slaves, Daniel and Nelson, also went back to the stable in case they were needed with the horses. This was the first time my youngest brother Bob had been to a funeral and he seemed to be quite upset by the death of Uncle Lucas.

After Uncle Lucas' funeral, Pa began to realize that running the inn made him a prisoner in his own home. He resolved to sell the inn and buy a cotton plantation when a good opportunity came along so he could have more freedom.

Opportunity came in 1846 and Pa sold the inn to Mr. David Terrell. Mr. Terrell was glad to get it, and Pa was glad to be rid of it even though the inn and stable had made a good living for us. After that, we lived in a rented house near Elim Baptist Church in the western part of Crawford County while Pa prospected for a plantation to buy in the former Indian Territory across the river. During that time, Pa rented out most of his slaves to local farmers, but he was always concerned that they might be mistreated. Pa's slaves were his most valuable possessions and he would never mistreat them any more than he would mistreat a fine horse.

While we were in our rented house we were quite active in Elim Church. Daniel and Nelson also became members of the church. Pa and I served on a variety of church committees and eventually Pa was elected a deacon and church treasurer. I suppose the most noteworthy thing I ever did for Elim Church was to deliver a speech on missions.

Naturally, I had a sweetheart. Her name was Susan Saphronia Howe and we called her Saphronia. She was from a well-established Crawford County family. Her grandfather had been a lieutenant during the Revolutionary War. When Saphronia and I realized that I would soon be leaving Crawford County for a new life across the river, we decided to hurry and get married so she could go with me. We were married in Elim Church by our new preacher, Brother A. T. Homes. Five of our slaves, Daniel, Nelson, Mose, Dock, and of course, Aunt Bessie, watched from the back rows as Saphronia and I exchanged our vows on Tuesday, February 2, 1847.

After the ceremony, the entire congregation celebrated with a covered dish dinner on the grounds. We made sure there were plenty of leftovers and after all the guests had eaten their fill, the leftovers were given to the slaves. It was a great day.

Several years later, when our children were coming along, we named our fourth child Homes after Reverend Homes, but he died when he was less than a year old.

Chapter 11

Pa Continues the Story

My son John Thomas told you about our life in Knoxville. Now I'm going to tell you about our removal from Knoxville to Macon County and about representing Macon County at the Georgia State Convention in Milledgeville. But first, I must tell you about my children, especially my four boys.

John Thomas is the eldest. He's already six feet, four inches tall, erect as an Indian, with a somewhat florid complexion. He's already showing signs of leadership and I expect great things from him. I suppose he's my favorite, but I try not to let it show. John Thomas has dark hair -- in fact, we all do -- and I suppose that's because of our Scotch-Irish ancestry. Both of my parents came over from Ireland when they were children.

James -- James Alston Carson, named after Martha's brother-in-law -- is my second son. I think he'll do well as a planter.

Joe Jr. -- Joseph Perryman Carson, named after a preacher -- is the one who's best at book learning. He likes poetry and history and things like that. Maybe he'll turn out to be a schoolmaster, or maybe even a lawyer. He's smart as a whip and a little bit strong-willed.

And Robert Hall Carson -- we call him Bob -- well, he's still just a boy, always happy, generous, and caring. If Joe is too strong-willed, maybe Bob is a bit too compliant. We'll see. It's too soon to tell much about Bob. You know how fast children can change.

As they got old enough, I gave each of the boys his own horse. James always rode his at full gallop where ever he went. One day a neighbor told me, "Joe," (my name is Joe like my son Joe Jr.), "that boy of yours is going to kill that horse."

I really don't like other people trying to mind my business. I replied, "When he does, I'll buy him another."

And the girls? I'm proud of them, too. They're growing up to be fine ladies. Someday I'll let their mother tell you about them.

Among the many travelers who passed by our inn were a man and his wife on their way to a new life somewhere in the West, perhaps Alabama or Mississippi. The man and his wife were not remarkable themselves, but their mode of transportation was. They had a horse and an ox. The woman was riding the horse, which also carried their small amount of camping gear behind the saddle. The man walked along driving the ox, which was pulling a hogshead (barrel) into which they had packed all their belongings. They had rigged up a horse collar, a pair of shafts, and an axle through the hogshead, so the hogshead rolled along behind the ox. When I was a boy, this was a fairly common means of transportation, but this was the first time I had seen anything like it in years. The man and his wife said they hoped to get to the Flint River before dark.

Seeing the ox gave Joe Jr. and Bob an idea. Why couldn't they use our cow to pull a wagon? The next Sunday they made up an excuse to stay home from church and as soon as we were gone, they proceeded to hitch the cow to the wagon. The noise of the wagon frightened the cow who ran away, overturned the wagon, and broke the harness. Joe and Bob had to chase the cow for almost a mile and lead her home. Of course cattle can be used as draft animals, but they have to be trained and the boys didn't know that.

Ma and I pretended to be upset when we found out what had happened, but actually, we thought it must have been funny. Ma said, "Boys will be boys."

John Thomas told you I went prospecting for land to buy in the former Indian territory. I was looking for just the right place with a ready-built house for me and my family, barns for the livestock, storage buildings for cotton and other crops, quarters for the slaves, and of course, cleared, fertile land so that I could start farming operations immediately. For two years I searched over much of Crawford and Macon Counties, mostly southward along the stage coach road from the Flint River Bridge near the old Benjamin Hawkins Indian Agency to Lanier in the former Indian Territory. Lanier was about thirty miles almost due south from Knoxville.

From Knoxville, the Federal Road passed the old Hawkins Indian Agency and the covered bridge across the Flint River. Immediately south of the bridge, the Federal Road turned westward, but the River Road branched off and continued southward toward the new railroad depot at the new town of Reynolds. South of Reynolds, the road passed several places which became important to us in our daily lives. In north-to-south order, they were The Troutman (or Carson) Place, Horse Creek, Wilburville, Tote Over Creek, Lanier, Miona Springs, and finally, Oglethorpe.

A field road led eastward through the swamp to the Bryan Ferry, and then on to the Bryan Place and Marshallville.

Jones Hicks' Mill and his White House lay on the west side of the River Road, upstream on Horse Creek.

An east-west road crossed the River Road at Lanier. It crossed the river via the Lanier Ferry (which later became known as the Marshallville Ferry) and continued on to Marshallville.

At that time, Lanier was the up-and-coming county seat of Macon County (not to be confused with the City of Macon), with a population of two hundred. However, after the railroad was built through Oglethorpe in the southern part of Macon County, Oglethorpe grew while Lanier declined. By 1870, Lanier had completely disappeared except for a modest cemetery. The stagecoach road south of the Flint River Bridge roughly paralleled the west side of the river along the edge of the swamp. That's why it was called the River Road.

On one of my prospecting journeys, I fell from my horse and was injured. Some field hands, property of Mr. Jones Hicks, found me and took me to the home of their master. Jones Hicks had a most impressive colonial style house built overlooking Horse Creek on his two- thousand-acre plantation atop the highest hill in the area. The house could be seen for miles around in all directions and it was called The White House because it was painted white. Mr. Hicks graciously admitted me to his home and cared for me while I recovered.

There was a vineyard and winery on the Hicks Plantation and Mr. Hicks produced some fine scuppernong wine. I can tell you from personal experience it was fine wine indeed. On the day that I left the Hicks Plantation, Mr. Hicks had imbibed a little too much. As I mounted my horse, he intended to say, "I'm sorry you were hurt, but I'm damn glad you were at my house." However, he got it twisted and said, "I'm glad you were hurt, and I'm damn sorry you were at my house." We both got a good laugh out of that. Jones and I became fast friends and later my daughter Mary Jane married Jones' son Rete, and my granddaughter Mattie married Jones' son Lewis.

While I was on the Hicks Place, Jones told me his neighbors, the Wilburs, were looking to sell their plantation. They were from up North somewhere, and considering the growing sentiment against Yankees, they were beginning to feel somewhat uneasy and felt that they should go back where they came from. The Wilburs made me an offer I could not turn down and soon I was the proud new owner of a plantation called Wilburville.

When I acquired Wilburville, I also acquired several field hands. They said, "We goes with the place."

The stagecoaches changed horses at Wilburville. I knew about running a stable for the stagecoaches, but the Wilburs also operated a big store and post office on their place. I wanted no part of the mercantile business because I knew it would be confining like the inn, so as soon as we got our first crop laid by, I sold the store building to William Minor. He tore it down and moved the lumber to Miona Springs where he used it to build a resort hotel. His Miona Springs Hotel became very popular because the waters of the seven different mineral springs were said to give relief from a variety of illnesses. The hotel even had a pavilion for dancing and a swimming pool lined with wooden boards. Most guests arrived at the hotel by stagecoach and a few came up the river on a small steamboat. The river was not navigable for the steamboat any further upstream because of rocks, snags, and sand bars. Sometimes a drought made the river not navigable and sometimes during a flood, the river grew from its usual 150-foot width to more than three miles in width, flooding the whole swamp.

Remember, this was new territory obtained from the Indians just thirty years earlier. Wolves could sometimes be heard howling in the distance. We often had to work around tree stumps in the fields. When the hands weren't busy in the cotton fields, I put them to work clearing more land.

One day our ten-year-old daughter Mary Jane attempted to cross Tote Over Creek on a log. She slipped and fell in. Two of our slaves, Daniel and Nelson, were cutting trees nearby. They heard Mary Jane's screams and pulled her out, otherwise she might have drowned. Daniel brought her home cold, wet, frightened, and embarrassed but otherwise unharmed. They told Ma what happened.

Ma said, "Thank you, Daniel, for bringing her home. I don't know what I'm going to do with that child. She's turning into a regular tomboy." Turning to Mary Jane, she added, "You run along and get out of those wet things, young lady, before you catch your death of cold, and don't wander off again like that, you hear?"

After just two years, the Troutman Place came up for sale. It had more land than Wilburville with a fine plantation house and many outbuildings on 2500 acres on the west bank of the Flint River. Ma and I sold Wilburville and bought the Troutman Place. Since our name is Carson, over the years the Troutman Place, complete with its single-story classical revival style house, became known as the Carson Place. Again, I put the hands to work in the cotton fields and clearing more land for crops. We also raised peaches, yams, pecans, peanuts, sugar cane, vegetables for our table, and corn and oats for the livestock, but cotton was our cash crop. I also permitted the slaves to plant vegetable gardens to supplement their rations. Each of them was permitted to keep chickens, and each year I gave each slave family a pig which they could raise and butcher in the Fall. We all hunted game such as deer and turkey in the Flint River Swamp and fished for bass, bream, and catfish in the river. Once in a while, someone would see a bear near our plantation and occasionally we heard reports of alligators in the river. Sometimes the slaves brought venison to the house and we always gave them some beef or pork in return, or perhaps an article of used clothing. Possum was an occasional part of the slaves' diet, but I never tried it.

The quarters – slave quarters, that is – were fifteen cabins arranged in a neat row behind the main house. The cabins were simple, two-room buildings with brick chimneys where the slaves slept on the dirt floor on pallets stuffed with straw or corn shucks. The windows had wooden shutters, there were no ceilings, and the roofs were wood shingles. Most of the slaves swept the sandy soil of their yards almost daily and did what they could to keep their homes neat and clean. They made their own repairs as necessary, but I supplied the materials. The slaves developed a strong sense of loyalty to their community.

We carried the hands to the fields every day in the wagon. Elderly slaves prepared the noon meal of peas, beans, turnips, potatoes, etc., all seasoned with a ham bone in a big iron pot, and we took this dinner in the wagon to the hands in the fields. Sometimes we supplied watermelons, okra, yams, rice, or peanuts, but very little meat. We rang the big farm bell when it was time for dinner to be over. In the evening, we went 'round to the fields in the wagon to gather the hands up for the ride home.

As far as clothing was concerned, twice a year I provided my slaves with store-bought cloth which they used to make their own clothes and my Martha taught them how to cut and sew the cloth. A few of the slaves also had cotton cards, spinning wheels, and looms in their cabins.

To make raw cotton into cloth, first the seeds must be removed, sometimes by hand but now most often in a cotton gin. Next, the cotton must be carded, that is, brushed or combed between a pair of cotton cards, stiff wire brushes with short bristles, to align the cotton fibers and to remove bits of trash such as leaves and twigs. Next, a spinning wheel is used to twist the fibers into yarn or thread, and finally the yarn or thread is woven into cloth on a loom. In inclement weather and when the crops were laid by, the female slaves carded, spun, and wove their own homespun cloth and sewed it into clothing. Usually two or three slaves worked together and took turns at the various jobs, and some of them became very skilled weavers and seamstresses.

I permitted my slaves to marry, but not all slave owners allowed slave marriages. I even attended most of the weddings which were always followed by feasting and dancing to fiddle and banjo music in the Quarter. However, the marriages had no legal status. I could have sold one spouse and kept the other, but I thought that would be especially cruel and I never did that to any of my slave families. Family relationships were very important in the slave community. Once or twice, one of my slaves wanted to marry someone from another plantation. In those cases, I sold my slave to the other plantation owner or bought his slave.

Our plantation did not have a body of water deep enough for baptisms, so the slaves dammed up a little creek in the swamp near the road to the Bryan Ferry. The dam burst during a hard rain, and the water gushing from the breach washed a big hole in the stream bed on the downstream side of the dam. This hole served as a place for baptisms just as well as the pond would have. The hole also became a favorite spot for swimming and fishing for both white and black children, and the hole is there to this day. Even though slave marriages had no legal status in Georgia, I expect the slave baptisms have status in Heaven.

According to law, slaves were not allowed to assemble except under supervision and it was illegal to teach a slave to read. On the other hand, the law supposedly protected slaves from abuse, but I never heard of any planter who was prosecuted under that law. Slaves were not allowed to testify at the trial of a white person, so it was difficult for slaves to prove abuse where it existed, and I'm sure it did exist on some plantations. By law, masters were required to receive approval of the Georgia Legislature before any slave could be set free, so manumission was impractical. The law required slave owners to care for old or infirm slaves.

The law required slaves to get permission from their masters whenever they left the plantation. I regularly granted such permission when my hands weren't needed in the fields and all my neighbors knew it so they seldom challenged my slaves. Sometimes my neighbors criticized me for my benign paternalistic treatment of the slaves, but I told them, "Mind your own business. How I treat my slaves is my business."

I made daily inspections of the plantation to make sure the crops were planted, cultivated, and harvested properly. It was very satisfying to watch the cotton plants sprout up from the ground in neat rows and grow to a height of three or four feet. Soon they developed buds called "squares", and then beautiful large white blossoms that turned a pinkish red in a few days. After the blossoms fell off, the bolls began to form, and after the bolls were fully formed they burst open to reveal the soft cotton fiber and seeds inside. The fiber was often damp from rain or dew, so we allowed it to dry and then it was cotton picking time. The plants continued to bear from early Autumn until the first killing frost, and sometimes there were open bolls near the bottoms of the plants while there were still blossoms near the tops.

The hands picked the cotton into cloth sacks with straps slung over their shoulders and when they reached the end of a row, they dumped the cotton onto large square pieces of burlap called cotton sheets. At the end of each day, they tied the four corners of the cotton sheets together and loaded them onto a wagon. The wagon took the cotton to our big barn. When we sold the cotton, we took it to either Reynolds or Oglethorpe, where a steam-powered gin removed the seeds and baled the fiber for shipment. Most of it was eventually sent to England or New England where it was made into cloth. We saved the seeds to plant the next year's crop.

We also used the burlap cotton sheets for other crops such as black eyed peas and okra.

The boys and I often took corn and wheat to Jones Hicks' mill where it was ground into grits, meal, and flour. The mill was on Horse Creek just down the hill from The White House. Jones had built an earthen dam across the creek to form the mill pond, about two acres in size, and there he had both a saw mill and a grist mill. The building for the grist mill stood on tall posts on the downstream side of the dam, accessible from the top of the dam by a little foot bridge. The machinery for the mill was unique, because instead of the usual overshot wheel found at most mills, the waterwheel at Hicks Mill was mounted beneath the building, and it was mounted horizontally on a vertical shaft. This greatly simplified the machinery because the shaft simply went straight up through the floor of the mill house to the mill stone which was directly above. With this arrangement, few gears were needed. Water came from the bottom of the dam, not the top, through a wooden conduit and struck one side of the horizontal water wheel, or turbine, tangentially with considerable pressure and produced more than enough power to turn the mill wheel above. I've never seen another mill made like Jones Hicks' mill.

We shucked and shelled our corn at home, put it into large cloth sacks, and carried it to the mill in a wagon. We drove the wagon onto the dam and stopped in front of the mill house. Daniel, or sometimes Nelson, carried the sacks of corn across the footbridge and upstairs to the second floor, where it was poured into a hopper. From there, it flowed from the hopper through a wooden chute down into the mill wheel on the first floor where it was ground into grits or meal and collected in cloth sacks. Dust covered everything in the mill, including the miller, and sometimes we couldn't even tell he was a black man. The miller kept part of our corn in payment for Mr. Hicks.

My wife Martha and our daughters made frequent trips in the buggy to Enoch Wilson's tailor shop in Lanier for things like fabric, ribbons, and thread, to Si Hill's grocery for supplies such as sugar and salt, and to the post office to pick up the mail. The post office at Lanier received mail deliveries by stagecoach from the railroad depot at Reynolds twice weekly. If a letter looked important, the postmaster sent it out by courier on a mule, but otherwise it simply waited until picked up. We were afraid to let Martha go to Lanier alone because of her epilepsy.

Martha loved to treat our important guests, especially those who stayed overnight, to lavish dinners. She set the table with our best china and silverware and loaded the table with ham, roast beef, and sometimes roast turkey, along with several different vegetables, stewed apples, cakes, and pies. After the ladies left the table, we men enjoyed our cigars with a little brandy.

We had barely got settled into the Carson Place when war came. It really didn't surprise anyone; war had been brewing for a long time. One of the first early warning signs came when the Methodist Church split because their Bishop Andrew, a Georgian, owned slaves and refused to give them up. In actuality, Bishop Andrew inherited his first slave from a couple in Augusta who asked Andrew to care for her until she was nineteen. Then he was to send her to Liberia, but she refused to go. The slave then lived in her own house on Andrew's lot in Augusta. Andrew said, "I have neither bought nor sold a slave, and in the state where I am legally a slaveholder, emancipation is impracticable."

Andrew's wife also owned several slaves, but Andrew himself was not their legal owner. At the Methodist General Conference of 1844, Andrew offered to resign his episcopacy, but the convention delegates from the Southern states would have none of it. They withdrew from the Methodist Church to form the Methodist Episcopal Church, South.

Another important cause of the war was that 1852 novel by Harriet Beecher Stowe. It helped fan Northern abolitionist ardor in the 1850's even though Stowe's book was a grossly exaggerated caricature of Southern slavery.

Of course, the war was about more than just slavery. There were issues like states' rights and protectionist tariffs, but slavery was the main issue. The economic system of the agricultural South was built almost entirely on slave labor. If the abolitionists had succeeded in abolishing slavery, how could we have maintained our way of life? If the free states had gained a majority in Congress, it would have been possible for the Yankees to run roughshod over the South, maybe even abolish slavery. We Southerners were becoming increasingly alarmed. We felt like we had our backs to the wall.

Most Southerners recognized the problem, but we did not all agree on the solution. As a result, the Democratic Party split into three factions with three different presidential candidates – John Bell of Tennessee, Stephen A. Douglas of Illinois, and John C. Breckenridge of Kentucky. The Republicans had only one candidate, Abraham Lincoln, who won the election of 1860 with only forty per cent of the popular vote and did not even appear on the ballots of ten Southern states.

The election of Abraham Lincoln in 1860 was the last straw. Now most of the Southern electorate began to coalesce around one solution – secession from the United States. Even many small farmers who did not own slaves supported secession because they felt the Yankees in Congress had been putting the interests of Northern merchants and bankers ahead of Southern farmers.

South Carolina declared its secession from the Union on December 20, 1860.

On January 2, 1861, Georgia held an election for representatives to the State Convention. Election Day was a miserable cold and rainy day so turnout at the poll was low. William H. Robinson of Lanier and I were selected to represent Macon County at the Convention.

The Georgia State Convention met in the Gothic-revival-style state capitol building at Milledgeville on January 16, presided over by former governor George W. Crawford. Some delegates, primarily from central and coastal parts of the state, were for immediate secession, while others, mainly from the mountains of North Georgia, preferred cooperation with the Federal Government provided certain conditions were met. When the vote was taken, the vote was 208-89 in favor of immediate secession. Since the vote was so one-sided, we voted again to make it unanimous. Then we all signed the Ordinance of Secession in an elaborate ceremony on January 19, 1861. Mississippi, Florida, and Alabama had already followed South Carolina into secession on January 9, 10, and 11, 1861, respectively, so our fair state of Georgia became the fifth state to secede. Six more states followed us, for a total of eleven.

Jefferson Davis was elected President of the Confederacy on February 9, 1861, and the first shots were fired at Fort Sumter, South Carolina, on April 12, 1861. The war had begun.

The Yankees will tell you that the South tried to secede. I say secession was an accomplished fact. We had our own government and constitution, our own army and navy, our own postal service, our own currency, and our own territory. We had our own Southern brogue and our own peculiar social custom (slavery). We were an independent nation, separate from the United States. In fact, in 1861 the Confederate States of America was the fourth wealthiest nation on earth. Territorial conquest was never our aim. The war we fought was purely a defensive war to protect our rights, our freedoms, and our way of life.

The Ordinance of Secession really amounted to Georgia's Declaration of Independence from the United States of America.

Chapter III

John Thomas Continues

My brother Joe and I both decided to join the Confederate Army, but it took me several weeks to convince Saphronia that it was my patriotic duty to join the army. Joe had no such encumbrance, so he was able to join about two months before me.

There were a number of Federal facilities on Southern soil -- courthouses, lighthouses, customs houses, forts, arsenals, mints, post offices, and the like. The *Macon Telegraph* newspaper told us President Davis sent a delegation to Washington with an offer to buy these facilities, but Abraham Lincoln refused to meet with the delegation. Instead, Lincoln issued a call for 75,000 volunteers (the maximum then allowed by Federal law) to augment the 16,000-man Union army for the purpose of capturing the Confederate Capitol at Richmond, Virginia. In response, the Confederate Congress issued a call for 100,000 volunteers to form an army to resist the anticipated Federal invasion. The response to the Confederate call for volunteers was immediate, and recruiting stations were swamped.

More than 750,000 individuals eventually served in the Confederate States Army, although not all at the same time. The Union army eventually grew to an authorized force of more than 500,000 men.

On June 15, 1861, I went across the river to Marshallville and enlisted into the Confederate Army for three years as a first lieutenant.

First Lieutenant John Thomas Carson, CSA -- I rather liked the sound of that.

Our captain was a former school teacher from Marshallville, Captain John McMillan. Our outfit was Company C, Twelfth Georgia Regiment, also known as the Davis Rifles in honor of our president, Jefferson Davis. Our motto was, "Jeff Davis and the South!"

Each of us signed an Oath of Allegiance, which read,

"I do solemnly swear or affirm that I will bear true allegiance to the State of Georgia, and that I will serve honestly and faithfully against all her enemies and opposers whatever, and observe and obey the orders of the Governor of the State of Georgia, and the orders of the officers appointed over me according to the rules and articles for the government of the troops of Georgia."

After each man had signed his oath of allegiance to the State of Georgia, we were issued our uniforms. They were all dyed a shade of light grey using vegetable dye, and included trousers, a high-collared double-breasted jacket, and a kepi hat with a brim made of cardboard and covered in oilcloth. The trousers had red stripes down the outseams designating infantry, and I received two embroidered collar patches with two gold bars indicating a first lieutenant. My buckle was a simple oval bearing the letters "CS." The army provided buttons for our jackets, but I preferred the Georgia buttons issued by the state with the state seal, by which I showed my loyalty to Georgia. After several months of hard use, our uniforms faded to a light brown color.

As an officer, I also received a dress sword, but Pa soon sent me a real sword imported from Germany. I have no idea where he got it or what he paid for it.

We reassembled in Marshallville three days later to take the train to Richmond. We really looked impressive in our new uniforms, and I had two extra uniforms that Saphronia and her house servants made for me. Ma, Pa, Saphronia, and all my brothers and sisters were in the crowd at the depot to see me off. The local band played a new song called "Dixie" as the train pulled away from the depot.

Richmond, Virginia, was the capitol of the Confederacy, but it was also important as an industrial center, transportation hub, and supply depot. The Tredegar Iron Works on the bank of the James River in

Richmond produced railroad rails and spikes, locomotives, stoves, and artillery pieces. Numerous smaller factories produced tents, uniforms, harnesses and other leather goods, swords, and bayonets. With a population of 38,000, Richmond was the second-largest city in the Confederacy, trailing only New Orleans.

In Richmond, we joined several other companies to form a regiment of about a thousand men and officially mustered into the Confederate Army in the Capitol Square.

Let me tell you about our introduction to military maneuvering.

On Sunday, July 7, 1861, we left Richmond by train for Staunton, Virginia and arrived there a little before daylight on Monday morning. We camped at Staunton overnight on Monday and on Tuesday morning we broke camp and began the march to Laurel Hill, about 125 miles away. The ladies of Staunton waved goodbye with their handkerchiefs, aprons, and bonnets from their windows, and their "God-speeds" cheered us greatly.

We marched about twelve to fifteen miles each day. Our regiment, with its long train of wagons following, was an impressive sight winding along the Virginia mountainsides on the rock-paved Staunton-Parkersburg Turnpike. Four mules pulled each wagon. Each mule required fourteen pounds of hay and nine pounds of grain per day, and they had to be fed even while we were in camp. Each wagon of rations included more than two tons of supplies such as bacon, beans, candles, coffee, flour, pork, rice, salt, etc. Other wagons carried surgeons' medical supplies, tents and baggage of the officers, and pots and kettles of the cooks. The wagons also carried forage for the animals, lubricants and spare parts, and of course, ammunition. These military wagons were heavy-duty wagons, much sturdier than regular farm wagons.

As we marched along, the muskets glistened in the sunlight. The march was very difficult for the men as most of them were not accustomed to such pedestrian exercise. We stopped at mid-afternoon on most days so that we could post guards, make camp, gather firewood, and make our suppers.

We all noticed there weren't any gnats in these mountains like we have down in Georgia -- a blessing. As a matter of fact, I've been told that the "gnat line" runs through Macon, Georgia, and there aren't any gnats north of this line.

After five days, we received word that a much-superior enemy force was advancing toward us from the opposite direction and had blocked the road between us and Laurel Hill. A retreat seemed the only prudent thing to do, so we retreated without firing a single shot nor seeing the enemy.

After a brief rest for supper, we marched all night and into the next day until we reached Monterrey, Virginia. When we reached our camp in Monterrey, the men simply dropped to the cold, damp ground and went to sleep with rocks for their pillows. I heard more than one man remark that he had never slept so soundly.

Soon we learned that the Federal army we had so feared was not so fearsome after all and had camped atop Cheat Mountain in western Virginia. We were ordered back toward Laurel Hill and set up a camp atop the Allegheny Mountains. From our camp we could sometimes see the enemy camp on Cheat Mountain, perhaps five or six miles away as the crow flies. We could see their campfires especially clearly at night and I suppose they could see ours, too.

General Robert E. Lee arrived in our camp in late July. After he personally scouted the enemy positions, he formed a plan to surround the Federals in their camp and attack. However, the order to attack never came, in part because of a very cold rain on the mountain, nearly impassable roads, and because about half our men were sick with measles. That rain was very cold and was most unusual for July, even for a mountain top. We sat by our fires in our overcoats. We got no help from local residents of the mountains as most of them were on the Union side. After some of our troops had a few skirmishes with the Yanks, which accomplished little, we withdrew to our base at Staunton. None of this made much sense to me. The only excuse for it that I could think of was that most of our commanders were as new to the army as I was. I was only a brand-new lieutenant, so I didn't complain. I kept my mouth shut and tried to learn.

After the non-battle of Cheat Mountain, the way was cleared for West Virginia to secede from Virginia and rejoin the United States as a separate state two years later.

We returned to Staunton and remained there for almost a year. The seat of Augusta County, Staunton was a most prosperous town with a population of four thousand and shops and warehouses filled to overflowing with the bounty of the Shenandoah Valley. Gas lights illuminated its main streets at night. Staunton's factories made carriages, wagons, boots, shoes, clothing, and blankets. Staunton was the home of the state insane asylum, the Institution for the Deaf, Dumb, and Blind, and newly-founded Staunton Military Academy.

The sudden arrival of our army more than tripled the population. The soldiers soon depleted all the merchandise in the shops, and re-orders were placed on back-order or completely unavailable. Shopkeepers sold out and merchandise for sale was reduced to thread and pins. Several hospitals were established to care for wounded and sick soldiers. The Institution for the Deaf, Dumb, and Blind was converted into a hospital that cared for both Confederate soldiers and Federal prisoners of war.

During our time there, many of our men found lodging in private homes. I sent for Mose to join me as a "body servant", or valet, and he brought a wagon-load of supplies with him.

In November of 1861 our officers brought us new battle flags. The old flag, the Stars and Bars, was deemed confusing from a distance in battle because it was too similar to the Federal flag. The new flag was a red square with two diagonal blue stripes crossing each other, and one white star representing each of the Confederate states on the blue stripes. Our officers told us to be proud of our new flag and not let it get soiled and never to surrender it. The new flag was called "The Stainless Banner."

Frankly, there was very little for the infantry to do at Staunton. We were bored. Most of us spent time writing letters to our homefolks and we looked forward to receiving mail from them. After several months, even drills, card games, band concerts, snowball fights (a new experience for us Georgians), and the pro-secessionist *Staunton Vindicator* newspaper seemed boring. We actually wished for a good fight.

We got our wish on the morning of May 7, 1862, when we received orders from General Stonewall Jackson to leave Staunton and march west along the Parkersburg Turnpike, which had been completed just twelve years earlier. We went to face a Union force led by General Milroy and we found some of their pickets at Roger's Tollgate. The pickets retreated so hastily that they left their baggage behind. The Yankees went first to the crest of Shenandoah Mountain and then to the town of McDowell.

The next morning we attempted to out-maneuver the Yankees. Realizing what we were up to, they fell back for a while, but about three o'clock they attacked and our Twelfth Georgia Regiment bore the brunt of it. Savage fighting ensued for four hours. Our regiment suffered 420 casualties partly because we were situated atop a ridge and so, silhouetted against the sky, made easy targets for the Yankee rifles. Their rifles were superior to our smooth-bore muskets. We could have fallen back to safety behind the ridge line, but we had not marched all the way from Staunton just so we could give ground before the Yankees, so we held the ridge. The Yankees were not able to break through our line, so about evening they withdrew. We chased them nearly to Franklin before returning to our base at Staunton.

Our regiment lost five lieutenants and five captains that day and I was promoted to captain to take the place of one of them, our own Captain McMillan. Mose sewed my new captain's bars onto my uniform.

Next we marched to New Market, Virginia where we joined up with General Ewell's forces on May 20, 1862. From New Market we marched to Massanutten Mountain and then to Luray, Virginia.

In Luray, we were joined by some soldiers dressed in brightly-colored uniforms with short, open-front jackets, brightly colored sashes around their waists and baggy pants, and they carried Model 1816 conversion muskets with socket bayonets. We were amazed at the way they pranced along and we couldn't understand where they got all that energy because we knew they had been marching all day long just as we had.

We learned that these soldiers in the strange uniforms were called Zouaves after a unit of the French army fighting in North Africa -- or the "Tiger Rifles" -- and they were from Louisiana. We also learned that they fought differently from us. They loaded their rifles lying on their backs and then rolled over into a prone position to fire. Also, they spread themselves out several feet apart when in battle instead of bunching up shoulder to shoulder like we did.

The Zouaves were an undisciplined, rowdy bunch when they weren't showing off, but they were also a very effective fighting force. They were often the first unit to attack the enemy. At one point they led a charge across a burning bridge and captured a train loaded with Federal supplies. I'm glad they were on our side.

After Luray we went to Front Royal, Virginia along the muddy Luray Road. Under the overall command of General Jackson, we engaged the Yankees in a lopsided victory at Front Royal on May 23, 1862 and almost seven hundred Yankees threw down their arms and surrendered. The rest were driven to Winchester, Virginia. We captured large amounts of supplies and weapons.

From Front Royal, we marched all night and arrived at Frederick County near Winchester, Virginia the next morning in a dense fog. We were exhausted. My regiment was mainly held in reserve, but the boys in other regiments took a great number of Yankee prisoners and captured so many supplies and wagons that we nicknamed General Banks, the enemy commander, "Commissary Banks."

During the fighting around Winchester, General Jackson ordered General Garnett's First Regiment to attack. The First Regiment began to run low on ammunition and were soon surrounded by Yankees on three sides. Seeing their situation, General Garnett ordered them to fall back without Jackson's permission. When General Jackson learned of Garnett's order to retreat, he pitched a conniption fit and had Garnett arrested for disobeying orders and neglect of duty. Only intervention by General Robert E. Lee saved Garnett from court-martial.

On May 30, we were back in Front Royal, guarding captured Federal arms and supplies when we were attacked by some Yankee cavalry. We were badly beaten and scattered, but we regrouped and Captain William F. Brown of Company F took command and led us back to Winchester where we camped near the Shenandoah River. We had marched so many miles and fought so many battles that we had begun to call ourselves the "Foot Cavalry."

While camped along the Shenandoah River I received a letter from Pa, who said that Ma had died of an epileptic seizure on June 21, 1862. Pa and the slaves dug her grave and buried her behind Pa's house. Pa marked her grave with a simple wooden cross and replaced it later with a marble headstone.

My brother James had enlisted in Company C on May 1. He and

I wanted to go home to comfort Pa, Saphronia, Melissa, Bob and our sisters, but we could not go because we could not get leave. We were busy with the defenses of the northern Shenandoah Valley. At least James and I were able to comfort each other a little, but our army duties prevented us from seeing each other very much.

General Robert E. Lee had given General Jackson, "Stonewall" as we called him, command of our forces in the Shenandoah Valley. As the war continued on, General Jackson was accidentally shot by some men from the Eighteenth North Carolina Regiment on the night of May 2, 1863. In the darkness, the North Carolinians shouted, "Halt! Who goes there?"

When Jackson's men frantically identified themselves, the North Carolinians' Major Barry said, "It's a damned Yankee trick! Fire!" and Jackson was struck three times. My brother Joe was assigned to drive the ambulance carrying General Jackson to the nearest railroad depot, a distance of thirty miles.

Jackson died on May 10. The newspapers quoted him from his deathbed: "I see from the number of physicians that you think my condition dangerous, but I thank God, if it is His will, that I am ready to go.… It is the Lord's Day; my wish is fulfilled.… I have always desired to die on Sunday." His body was taken to Richmond for a period of public mourning, and then taken to Lexington, Virginia, for burial. General Garnett served as a pall bearer and wept openly at Jackson's funeral, despite the fact that Jackson had tried to have him court-martialed earlier. Garnett was Jackson's brother-in-law.

In October of that same year I learned that my Pa had remarried. My new mother was Mary Laura Slappey, a widow from Marshallville just across the River from the Carson Place. I was quick to write to my brothers and sisters at home, saying "Glad to learn that the children are pleased with their new mother. I hope she will become a mother indeed to all of us. Let each one strive to render her happy as well as to add to Pa's happiness. I hope that he may spend the remainder of his days as comfortable and happy as it be possible for a companion and dutiful children to render him…."

Winchester, Virginia was a transportation hub. It was the meeting point of three railroads, seven major highways, and a canal. Almost ten thousand Union soldiers had re-occupied Winchester almost as soon as we left in May of 1862. They threatened the northern Shenandoah and in June of 1863, it was high time we sent them home again.

After Major Hawkins was promoted to lieutenant colonel, I was promoted to major on June 9, 1863 and just four days later I found myself in another battle at Winchester. The night before the battle, a strong storm arose and drenched us and the city of Winchester all night long. But it cleared up before dawn and at six o'clock we attacked the Yankees on Bower's Hill. The Yankees retreated. Under the command of General John B. Gordon, our brigade and two batteries were left to hold the hill while General Early's forces executed a flanking maneuver behind some hills and out of sight of the Federals. Our batteries soon began firing on the Federals at Fort Milroy and the ensuing artillery duel lasted until mid-afternoon.

While the artillery battle was in progress, some of Early's men occupied a corn field below the enemy position without being seen by the Yankees on the hill. Late in the afternoon, Early's men suddenly rushed Fort Milroy from their cornfield, captured the enemy guns, planted the flag of secession on the hill, and turned the cannons around to use against the fleeing Yankees.

During that night, the Federals abandoned all of their positions so quietly that we were not aware they had gone until morning. General Early's men discovered the retreating Yankees and attacked. Their general's horse was shot out from under him and his men scattered in all directions. Our forces captured four thousand prisoners, twenty-three pieces of artillery and three hundred loaded wagons, more than three hundred horses, and a large amount of commissary and quartermaster stores, enough to equip a battalion. The prisoners included the Federal wounded who were hospitalized in Winchester. About twelve hundred Yankees, including General Milroy, escaped to Harper's Ferry. We lost only 269 men, so this was one of the most lopsided victories of the war.

At Harper's Ferry, the Yankees arrested General Milroy for ignoring an order to withdraw from Winchester and move his troops to Harper's Ferry. As a result of ignoring the order, he had lost most of his troops and supplies. Our side put the supplies to good use. In addition, the loss of his troops meant that the important Federal Arsenal at Harper's Ferry was not well defended.

While the Federal troops had occupied Winchester, the Yankees tried to set the citizens of Winchester -- and indeed, civilians throughout the Shenandoah Valley -- against one another by telling the poor that the rich had caused the war and were the cause of all their miseries. This attempt at propaganda didn't work.

The Federal troops had rudely mistreated the ladies of Winchester, so as the Union army retreated through town a few of the ladies tried to get even by taking potshots at them from second-story windows.

We followed up our victory at Winchester with an advance up the Shenandoah Valley into Pennsylvania with General Lee and General Gordon. On the way, we were ordered to capture Harrisburg, Pennsylvania, if possible, and the only way to Harrisburg lay through Wrightsville and across the Susquehanna River over a mile-long wooden covered bridge, the longest covered bridge in North America..

General Gordon gave us orders not to damage civilian property if it could be avoided. However, the night before our advance into Wrightsville, we could find no firewood for cooking, and asked the General for permission to use wooden rails from an old-fashioned wooden fence. General Gordon told us to take the top rails only, but by morning the farmer's entire fence had disappeared.

The next morning the retreating Yankees set fire to the bridge. That stopped our advance, and there wasn't a pail or bucket anywhere to be found that we could use to extinguish the fire. Wind-blown embers from the burning bridge set fire to a lumber yard in Wrightsville and then to the town itself, and the town would have been totally destroyed if General Gordon hadn't ordered us to work side-by-side with the Yankee civilians to extinguish the blazes. Suddenly the civilians found plenty of buckets for us to use, and after four hours the fires were all extinguished. Since our path to Harrisburg was blocked, we rejoined the rest of Lee's army the next morning and continued through the Shenandoah Valley.

We arrived at Gettysburg on sultry July 1, 1863. About three o'clock in the afternoon, yelling deafeningly, our regiment attacked the Union Eleventh Corps and drove them from a little hill called Barlow's Knoll (named for their general) and we were able to hold the knoll in the face of three or four half-hearted Union counterattacks.

As the Yankees were retreating from our attack, Yankee General

Barlow was wounded twice. He fell to the ground and was left by his men for us to find. General Gordon recognized Barlow as he lay on the ground, and dismounted from his horse to speak with him. Gordon assumed that Barlow was going to die and asked, "Is there anything I can do for you?"

Barlow replied, "Yes, can you get a message to my wife and tell her what has happened?"

"I can and I will," replied Gordon.

Gordon ordered that Barlow be taken to a Confederate field hospital which had been set up in a farmhouse where he was cared for until we withdrew. I heard a rumor that Mrs. Barlow was allowed safe passage through our lines to visit her husband, but I don't know if that's true. We heard lots of rumors in the army.

Another rumor was that four women disguised themselves as men and fought alongside our men at Gettysburg. The rumor said that two of them were killed and two were discovered and sent to Castle Thunder Prison in Richmond, the only Confederate prison where women were kept. The women were eventually set free. After all, what law had they broken?

Other Confederate units, led by General Pickett, vigorously attacked the Yanks over the next two days, but the Yanks held their ground so overall the battle was more or less a draw.

Robert E. Lee had saved General Garnett from court-martial under General Jackson and Garnett was still trying to re-establish his reputation. Leading his brigade, he bravely but ill-advisedly rode his horse into enemy gunfire and was killed on July 3, the last day of the battle.

Fighting at Gettysburg had subsided by July 4. It was raining and we stared at the enemy across the bloody battlefield watching men from both sides gather their dead and wounded under white flags of truce. We waited for a Union counterattack that never came. We actually hoped for a counterattack. We would have whipped them badly.

Seeing that there was nothing more to be gained by further slaughter, General Lee ordered us to withdraw in the evening of July 4 and we slipped away in the night. General Barlow was left behind in a tent where he was soon found by Union soldiers. He remained in a Union army hospital for several months and eventually made a full recovery.

Our wagon train was more than ten miles long with our wounded in ambulances and wagons in the front, headed for hospitals in Lynchburg. Mose drove one of the wagons from a saddle astride the left rear mule, or "wheeler." A steady pull on the single rein and a shout of "Haw!" turned the team to the left, short jerks and a shout of "Gee!" turned the team to the right, and a shout of "Yay!" meant straight ahead. Mose also operated the wagon's brakes from his saddle. This was quite different from driving a wagon on our farm at home.

Horses are faster than mules and are less skittish at the sound of gunfire, so horses are almost universally used for cavalry and are preferred for pulling ambulances. However, mules are stronger than horses and therefore better suited for pulling heavy loads. Someone told us that a group of Yankee soldiers suggested promoting their mules to the rank of "horse." I wish we had thought of that because our mules certainly earned some extra recognition.

We had extra horses and mules with us and about three thousand sorely-needed head of cattle that we had confiscated from Pennsylvania farms. Each beef would supply meat for five hundred men for one day. They were rations on the hoof.

General Imboden's cavalry defended our rear as we made our way south. Union cavalry units harassed the rear of our column, but the main Union army was unable to catch up to us.

As we passed through the town of Greencastle, our wagon train was attacked by a group of about fifty civilians with axes. They smashed wheels of twelve of our wagons before Imboden's cavalry drove them away.

The rain came down in torrents and flashes of lightning temporarily blinded the mules. Driving the mules became very difficult, but we had to keep moving. The road became a sloppy muddy mess and a few of the horses and mules simply dropped dead from pulling their heavy loads through the mud. Many of the axles on our vehicles broke, especially axles of the artillery carriages. As if to add insult to injury, we learned that Vicksburg, Mississippi had fallen to the Yankees on July 4. We were a very despondent, demoralized army as we marched south.

The wagons full of wounded soldiers had no springs, and most did not even have a bed of straw. Whenever a wagon went over a bump, the wounded passengers would cry out, "Oh, God, why can't I die? My God, will no one have mercy on me and kill me? Stop! For God's sake, stop for just a moment! Take me out and leave me on the roadside to die!"

As a matter of fact, we did leave a few of our most severely wounded soldiers on the roadside, where we hoped that local civilians would find them and take care of them.

The Potomac River was swollen by the rain. The cold water was up to our armpits and our comrades who were short of stature had great difficulty in crossing it, but we managed to ford the river while the cavalry held the Yankees at bay. We were grateful that we were still alive and at last we were on Southern soil. The gloomy spirit left us and our fighting spirit began to return.

We returned to our former positions near Winchester where we continued to guard against Yankee incursions into the Shenandoah Valley in Virginia.

When all the figures became available, newspaper reports said we lost 22,638 men killed, wounded, or missing while the Yankees lost 17,684. Besides the human losses, the two armies together also lost some fifteen hundred horses and mules. We heard that the residents of Gettysburg gathered all the dead horses and mules and burned them, and the stench made people sick for miles around.

Our losses were only slightly more than the Yankee losses, but what was almost an even exchange actually worked to an advantage for the Yanks because they had more replacements than we had.

Historians will say the Battle of Gettysburg was a tremendous victory for the Union Army because we left the battlefield first, but I think the Battle of Gettysburg was actually an inconclusive draw.

Chapter IV

James Begins His Story

I married a girl from a plantation across the river – Melissa Bryan -- and she was glad to become Mrs. James Alston Carson. Our wedding date was Tuesday, January 29, 1856. She was not yet eighteen, I was twenty-three. The wedding was held at the Bryan Place, perhaps the first house built in Macon County sometime about 1833. It was a two-story "dogtrot" house with one large room on either side of an open-ended central hall and a porch across the front of the house. It was situated on the ridge overlooking the Flint River Swamp with a view that extended westward for miles and miles. You could even see the Carson Place and the White House from the Bryan home. Ma, Pa, and all my family attended our wedding, as did all of Melissa's family.

The Bryans were very prosperous. At one time they operated a slave market. Many of the slaves were brought down from the North because the Yankees had begun to believe the weather in the North was too cold for profitable slavery. The Yankees also knew that slave trading was very profitable even though importation of African slaves into the United States had been illegal since 1808. The wealth of many prominent New England families was based on the slave trade. I'm sure the Yankees enjoyed the money they got by selling their slaves to us.

Melissa's father was the first banker in Macon County. He kept money under his bed and lent it to his neighbors. He also operated a stagecoach stop and his four-thousand-acre plantation. I was very fortunate to marry into such an industrious, prosperous family.

After three years Melissa and I were able to purchase 120 acres of land and a house where we set up our own housekeeping.

Everyone thought the war would soon be over because the legal arguments for secession were strong and no one believed the North had any stomach for fighting. After all, what we did in the South was our business, not theirs. What right did the Yankees have to tell us how to live? President Davis said it best: "All we ask is to be let alone."

Georgia's Governor Brown was an especially strong advocate for states' rights and individual freedom, and although the Confederate Government tried to impose a military draft, Governor Brown did not enforce it in Georgia. The draft was a detestable Yankee thing.

But as the war progressed, it became obvious that the war would be a long and bitter struggle, and every available man would be needed if we were to keep our independence. Melissa, Bob, Ma, and Pa went with me to Oglethorpe where I made my will and volunteered as a private in Company C, Twelfth Georgia Regiment, on May 1, 1862. That was the same company that John Thomas was in. We departed immediately for Richmond, Virginia.

My youngest brother Bob wanted to join the army like John Thomas, Joe Jr., and me but Pa said he was too young. He was only sixteen.

In Richmond, I was issued a Springfield Model 1853 musket with a rifled bore, along with forty Minie balls, black powder cartridges, and percussion caps. I'm no marksman, but those who are can hit a three-foot-diameter bullseye at nine hundred yards using a Springfield Model 1853. Maximum range for this gun is said to be two thousand yards, much better than a smooth-bore musket. A number of copies of this gun were manufactured in Richmond, but I received one made in England. It was a very fine weapon, ideal for killing Yankees, and I was proud to have it. It weighed nine and one-half pounds. I carried clean clothing, food, and other supplies in my knapsack, and my bedding rolled up across my shoulders in addition to my rifle. Altogether, I must have had about fifty pounds to carry. My pay was eleven dollars per month, and it was always late.

Although I was not a good marksman, the men of Company C

must have recognized my other abilities because they elected me third sergeant (June 15, 1862) and then second sergeant (July 8, 1862), and my pay was raised to seventeen dollars per month. I fought with Generals Robert E. Lee and Jubal Early in and around Richmond and Petersburg, Virginia.

I learned to eat hardtack, which we all carried in our rucksacks because it was cheap and didn't spoil. Hardtack was a simple cracker, just flour and water mixed and rolled to a thickness of about three eighths of an inch, poked with a fork to speed baking and cut into squares. We said it was "indestructible, imperishable, practically inedible, too hard to chew, too small for shoeing mules and too big to use as bullets." One of our boys said he found a soft spot in a piece of hardtack -- it was a nail. I learned to eat it, but I never learned to like it.

Nearly all of us liked coffee, the stronger the better. Some of us liked it strong enough to float a horseshoe. Sometimes, when our officers weren't watching, the boys swapped some of our tobacco for some of the Yankees' coffee -- that is, when they weren't shooting at each other.

When we were on the march we carried our bedding rolled up across our shoulders. The Yankees, I learned, carried theirs inside their knapsacks which were larger than our knapsacks.

Soon we were sent to guard the railroad interchange at Gordonsville, Virginia, about sixty miles northwest of Richmond. There I contracted something like influenza or bilious fever and was sent to a hospital that had been set up in the Exchange Hotel at Gordonsville, newly rebuilt after a fire just two years earlier, and I remained there for several days. John Thomas said many new recruits get sick soon after they join the army, and he thought it was because they were not accustomed to camp life.

I had been in the army less than four months, and I was eager to return to my unit. It was imperative that we prevent the Yanks from capturing Gordonsville, because the railroads that met at Gordonsville connected the agricultural cornucopia of the Shenandoah Valley and Charlottesville to the Confederate capital at Richmond.

Chapter V

Pa Tells about the Death of James

One day the courier from Lanier brought Melissa a letter from John Thomas. He wrote that James had returned to his army duties before completely recovering from his illness and had collapsed on the battlefield during a fight at a place called Cedar Run during a merciless heat wave on August 9, 1862. James had been taken to a hospital in Lynchburg, where he passed away

John Thomas' letter said the Yankees attacked our men about five o'clock on that hot afternoon, and our men fell back until Stonewall Jackson rode onto the scene. Jackson attempted to pull his saber from its scabbard, but found that it was rusted into the scabbard because he used it so seldom. He unbuckled the saber and brandished it above his head -- scabbard, belt, and all -- and rallied the men. Then our troops charged and the Yankees fell back, and James collapsed during the charge. As nightfall approached, Jackson called a halt to the pursuit. After two more days of skirmishing, the Yankees withdrew from the entire area around Gordonsville.

His body was returned to us and we buried him behind my house near his mother. May he rest in peace.

Later, John Thomas sent us a newspaper clipping that said casualties at Cedar Run were 2353 Union soldiers (314 killed, 1445 wounded, and 594 missing) and 1338 Confederates (231 killed, and 1107 wounded).

Joe Jr. Begins His Story

My name is Joseph Perryman Carson. Sometimes people call me "Joe Junior" to distinguish me from my Pa.

I was the first of our family to go to college, graduating with a Bachelor of Arts degree from Mercer University at Penfield, Georgia, in 1860. The university had several impressive buildings, most notably the Greek-revival-style chapel, and the town of Penfield had grown up around the University. There was a female academy, male academy, post office, bank, mercantile stores, print shops, hosiery mill, cotton warehouses, and residential housing surrounding the campus. The people who owned the private homes were required to provide housing for the university students.

Ma and Pa and my whole family came to see me receive my diploma; they filled up two whole rows of seats at the ceremony. It was a great day.

Most of the senior classes of 1861 and 1862 joined the army, as did most of the alumni, to "defend their constitutional rights and sacred honor."

Rete Hicks and I enlisted in the Army of the Confederacy as a privates in Company I (The Macon County Volunteers), Fourth Georgia Regiment, on April 29, 1861 under Captain Samuel Prothro, M.D. Actually, we enlisted just about two months before John Thomas enlisted. After a year, the men of Company I elected me first lieutenant.

We served on picket duty near Richmond and got into several skirmishes with the Yanks in June, but really saw no major battles there.

I was appalled by the foul language used by many of our boys. Some of them seemed unable to put two sentences together without the use of curse words. But as the war dragged on, they began to see what happened to some of their friends and messmates, and they realized the same thing might happen to them. After a year or so of war, many of our back-sliding soldiers began to attend religious services whenever possible and the use of foul language decreased sharply.

There was a resurgence of religion in the civilian population also, and the folks back home made sure we had plenty of tracts to read. Those tracts were the only reading material many of us had. Most local preachers (and politicians) back at home believed that God favored the Southern cause and said so in their sermons. We all believed that Southern slavery was ordained by God, and it was our duty to Christianize the African slaves.

Black preachers on the plantations usually preached about obedience and submission, but when their white masters were out of earshot they preached that one day the Lord would set them free.

I wanted a "body servant" like my brother John Thomas, so I sent for Dock to join me in Virginia and Dock considered it a great honor to be chosen for this duty. I put him to work cooking, doing laundry, cleaning my quarters, running errands, and foraging for corn and other supplies. When he wasn't working for me, I allowed him to earn a little money by working for other officers. Like Mose, Dock arrived with a wagon-load of supplies, some for me and some for other members of Company I.

Shortly after Dock arrived, the army headed for Maryland. General Lee wanted us to find supplies in Maryland and so relieve Virginia from having to support our army. As we marched along we sang "Maryland My Maryland," and even General Lee was overheard singing that song.

I was a first lieutenant at Sharpsburg, Maryland, on September 17, 1862 when my unit defended the Sunken Road, or "Bloody Lane," a mere thirty-five miles south of the Federal capitol of Washington, D. C. The Sunken Road was a farm lane that farmers used to bypass Sharpsburg. Over the years, rain and the wheels of farmers' wagons had worn the road down two or three feet below the surrounding ground level, so it was a natural defensive position. We reinforced this position with fence rails piled along the embankment and waited for the Yankees.

The Yankees attacked us about nine thirty in the morning. When they had advanced to within a hundred yards of our position, we let loose a volley that set them back temporarily, but they quickly resumed their attack and furious fighting ensued. We had a strong defensive position, but we were seriously outnumbered and we were forced to withdraw about one o'clock. However, the Yankees were too exhausted to pursue us. In this morning of fighting, about 5500 men were killed and neither side gained an important advantage. The Battle of the Sunken Road was just one part of the Battle of Sharpsburg.

Fifty-five-year-old General Lee had been injured in a fall from his horse a few days earlier, but despite a sore shoulder and bandaged hands, he stationed himself atop a hill with a view of the battle and directed his troops from that vantage point.

The Battle of Sharpsburg, which included the Sunken Road, was the single bloodiest day of the war up to that point, and later I learned that there were more than 22,000 casualties in both armies combined and we lost more than one-fourth of our entire army at Sharpsburg.

During the night of September 18, General Lee ordered us to withdraw across the Potomac River into Virginia and the Shenandoah Valley to forage for much-needed supplies. We also received clothing, shoes, ammunition, and rifles that General Jackson and his men had captured from the federal arsenal at Harper's Ferry. A number of our boys were barefoot, so the shoes were particularly appreciated.

The Yankees rested on their side of the river in Maryland and claimed victory because we had withdrawn, but I think we won because we had slightly fewer casualties than the Yankees.

After the so-called Union victory at the Battle of Sharpsburg, Lincoln issued his "Emancipation Proclamation." Issuing the Proclamation was a shrewd political move for Lincoln. Northern support for the war was flagging because of the large number of casualties, and the Proclamation greatly increased Northern popular support for the war. However, it had very little immediate effect in the South because Lincoln's authority did not extend into the Confederacy.

General Gordon was one of the casualties. He was rushed to a makeshift hospital which had been set up in an old barn.

When Mrs. Gordon was allowed in to see him, she had to stifle her scream. He had been struck twice in the leg, once in the left arm, once in the shoulder, and once in the face. He was lying on a bed of straw. His face was black, his jaw was wired shut, his arm had been amputated, and he was covered in bandages. Mrs. Gordon had to feed him liquids because his jaw was wired shut. When the bandages were removed, Doctor Weatherly found that he had erysipelas, a skin disease. Doctor Weatherly said that if he were to survive, Mrs. Gordon would have to paint him in iodine several times a day. She did this faithfully until he was fully recovered.

I was also one of the wounded, but my wound was not very serious and I was eager to get back into action.

After I had been out of the hospital just a few days, a messenger came to my tent and said, "Lieutenant sir, Major Carson over at the Twelfth Regiment wants to see you right away."

The major was my brother, John Thomas. At his tent his sentry saluted. I returned the salute and stepped inside.

"Sit down, Joe," John Thomas said, motioning me toward a folding camp chair. "I've arranged for you to be transferred to the Twelfth Regiment for a few days and I've got a special assignment for you."

"What's that?" I asked.

He said, "You know, or maybe you don't know, that I've been concerned about my children. They may not be getting a proper education. I love Saphronia dearly, but she's simply not cut out to be a teacher. Saphronia realizes it too and she has asked me to find a tutor for the children. Besides, she's got all she can say grace over trying to run the farm."

"Wait a minute!" I said. "I'm in the army. I can't just up and leave and go home to teach your kids. I've got a job to do here!"

John Thomas cut me off. "I know that," he said, "and I'm not asking you to become a schoolmaster. But look at this notice in the paper," and he produced a copy of the Lynchburg *Daily Republican* from his desk.

I read the advertisement, and said, "So? This Miss Charlotte Briggs wants to be a nanny or school teacher or something. What does that have to do with me?"

My brother the major said, "I've already discussed this with your new major, Major Winn. He agreed, so I've arranged a twenty-day furlough for you. Miss Briggs has agreed to go to Georgia to look after my kids and act as their tutor until the war is over and I want you to take her to Georgia. She thinks she'll be safer in Georgia and I think she'll be good for my kids. She's staying at a hotel in Lynchburg and you can meet her there. Besides, Major Winn and I think you need a little more time to recover from your wound."

"But, sir," I started to say, but he cut me off again.

"Get back here as soon as you can, Joe. We need good officers like you. Dismissed!" he said. I stood and saluted and his return salute ended our meeting.

Escorting an old maid schoolteacher to Georgia was not what I wanted to do. However, orders were orders, so I went to meet this Miss Briggs. But I just went in my regular uniform. I didn't bother to bathe or shave or brush my hair. I didn't want to impress anybody, I just wanted to get this interruption over as quickly as possible so I could return to my unit. I was dirty and sweaty and smelly and I really didn't care.

Imagine my surprise when Miss Briggs turned out to be an absolutely beautiful twenty-five year old, beautifully dressed, educated, cultured, poised, and self -confident without seeming pushy or arrogant. I was astounded that my brother could find such a perfect lady in the midst of this war.

I introduced myself. Miss Briggs looked me over and hastily decided not to go anywhere with such a dirty soldier. She said, "I suppose your brother sent you. Please tell him I've decided to stay here in Lynchburg, so I won't be going to Georgia after all."

I was flabbergasted, but I regained my composure enough to say, "Please reconsider, because I know my brother will be greatly disappointed to hear that. I'll come back this evening, and you can give me your final answer then."

Back in camp, I found Dock and said, "Quick, Dock, it's an emergency! I need that new uniform and those new boots I've been saving. Draw me a bath and get my shaving kit. Don't take time to heat the water for the bath, just a little hot water for shaving. I'll bathe in cold water. Where's the soap? And bring me a towel. While I'm gone, you can wash this old uniform for me. Oh, and make sure my horse has some oats and some water, and bring me one of those calling cards I showed you."

In thirty minutes I looked and felt like a new man. Dock said, "My, my, ain't you sumpin? You must be goin' courtin', 'cause it ain't time for church, Master Joe."

"I am, Dock, I am," was all I said.

When I returned to Miss Briggs' hotel I sent my calling card to her room, and when she came back downstairs it was her turn to be amazed. There I was, bathed and clean-shaven, and in the new uniform and boots of a junior officer in the Army of the Confederacy. She said she could hardly believe I was the same man she had seen earlier in the day.

We chatted about the war and the weather for a few minutes and then she said, "I'm surprised you were able to get back here so soon. Isn't your camp all the way across town?"

"Yes ma'am, it is, but I told Dock I needed to get cleaned up in a hurry and he was a big help. It helps to have a good horse, too," I explained. "I apologize for the way I looked this morning."

"Who's Dock?" she asked.

"Several of us have valets," I explained, "and he's mine. I sent for him when I was promoted to lieutenant. My brother has a valet named Mose. The army calls them 'body servants'"

"Well," said Miss Briggs, "I think I will go with you to Georgia after all. Please tell your brother."

"Good," I replied. "Have your things ready in the morning. It will be a long trip, but I think we'll be just fine."

In the morning, I made a brief report to John Thomas and then Dock and I made the trip into Lynchburg in the wagon. I met Miss Briggs at her hotel. Her trunk was already packed and waiting for us in the hotel lobby.

Dock loaded the trunk into the wagon and headed to the busy brick depot with its twin towers while Miss Briggs and I walked. It wasn't very far and it was a pleasant morning so we didn't mind at all. I bought a one way ticket for her and a round trip ticket for me.

Most of our ten thousand miles of railroad were built to move cotton from the interior to the ports, and passenger service was a sort of step-child or afterthought.

Our train was crowded with soldiers, some with crutches and bandages, and some simply going home for a much-needed rest. The train was showing signs of wear and tear from overuse and poor maintenance during the war. Supplies for maintenance were in short supply. Many of the skilled railroad maintenance workers had been Yankees who went back home at the beginning of the war and others were Southerners who left their railroad jobs to join the army. During the war, the railroads gave the army priority over everything else and because very little cotton was sent to the blockaded ports, railroad revenues were drastically reduced.

In places we slowed to a crawl because the track was not in good condition and once we stopped so the train crew could cut firewood for the locomotive.

My officer's uniform earned us special privileges so we were able to have a seat the entire journey. The scenery seemed to fly by. We spent the time talking. She told me about her childhood and her adventures on the western frontier while her father was a missionary there, and then about her life in boarding school in Lynchburg. I told her all about our farm and my family, and of course, she wanted to know about the children. Then I told her about life at Mercer University and in due time we were in Chattanooga.

We changed trains in Chattanooga and hired a carriage to transport us and our luggage across town to the next depot. This train was a little nicer, but still somewhat grimy with ashes and smoke from the locomotive. The conductor was a tall, slender, elderly gentleman who came around to check our tickets periodically. As day turned into night, the conductor lit the lamps in the car and we fell asleep in our seats. Besides the normal stops at depots to take on firewood and water, we only stopped twice to allow north-bound trains full of military supplies and recruits to pass and we didn't encounter a single cow on the tracks.

Eventually we pulled into Atlanta's Union Station with its tangle of five-foot gauge tracks headed in all directions. We caught the Macon and Western Railroad to Macon, and after that, the Western Railroad to Fort Valley, and then the Muscogee Railroad west to Reynolds. At Reynolds we hired a horse and buggy from the livery stable, and in another hour we were home.

Over the next several days, I spent as much time with Charlotte as I could. I introduced her to the family. I showed her the barns and the slave quarters and the pump house and the smoke house. We rode over the fields to examine the crops of cotton and corn, and I showed her the vegetable garden, the wash house, and the hen house.

In the late afternoon of my last day at home, I took her on a little picnic, just the two of us. While we were on the picnic, I proposed marriage to her and to my surprise and delight, she accepted! I hadn't had time to buy a ring, but she said she didn't mind. When we got back home, Pa said, "Well?" and we told him the good news. We must have been pretty obvious.

I don't remember much about my trip back to the army. I think I must have floated.

Chapter VII

Pa

My son John Thomas told you that I lost my Martha to an epileptic seizure in June of 1862 and that I remarried five months later to the day. John Thomas didn't tell you how lonely I was in the meantime. I kept my loneliness hidden from my daughters, from my youngest son Bob, and from my daughters-in-law Saphronia and Melissa. Besides, John Thomas was away at the war. He couldn't have known.

Mary was a widow and a Baptist like me. Her husband had been dead for several years, and her sons Reuben and William were away at the war like my sons, so she was just as lonely as I was. When I met Mary, she was struggling to manage her farm alone and I began to offer advice. Very soon we realized that we were kindred souls made for each other and my trips to her farm across the river near Marshallville became more and more frequent.

I went in the buggy and I always took Daniel or Nelson along to drive the buggy and to pull the ferry, known as Bryan's Ferry, across the river. The ferry was really a simple affair, not much more than a raft made of logs with planks nailed on top to form a deck. There were two pulley blocks attached to the upstream side of the raft, one at each end. A strong rope across the river passed through the pulley blocks and was tied to a stout tree on either side of the river; this arrangement kept the raft from floating downstream. There were also two more ropes, one tied to each end of the raft. Each of these ropes was long enough to reach all the way across the river, and they were also tied to trees on the river banks. They were used to pull the ferry across the river and they could be pulled hand-over-hand by someone aboard the craft or by someone on the shore. Ours was not the only such ferry along the river. There were similar ferries all up and down this section of the river. The Lanier Ferry (sometimes called the Miona Ferry) downstream on the road from Lanier to Marshallville was open to the public.

There were not any ferries like this below Miona Springs. Ropes could not be tied across the river below Miona Springs because the river had to be kept open for the small steamboat that occasionally served the Miona Springs Hotel.

One day as Daniel and I approached the ferry in the buggy, a man came out of the swamp and waved for us to stop, and we saw by his uniform that he was a Yankee soldier. He said that he had been assigned to a prison detail at Andersonville Prison to gather firewood outside the stockade. He had escaped and was trying to get back to the Union lines but the distance was much farther than he thought. He said he had no food nor water, had been unable to catch any game nor find any edible nuts or berries, and the water from the muddy river was not fit to drink. He said he needed help as he was thirsty and starving.

We were happy to oblige. We took him into the buggy. The river current pulled the ferry into the middle of the river; then Daniel took over, pulling us to the far side while I held my gun on our prisoner. We delivered him to the constable in Marshallville who gave him something to eat and then sent him back to Andersonville.

Chapter VIII

John Thomas

After the battle of Gettysburg, the next action I saw was at Spottsylvania Courthouse in May of 1864. Abraham Lincoln had given the Yankees two objectives: Capture the Confederate Capitol at Richmond, and destroy the Confederate army. As part of that overall strategy, the Yankees were bent on capturing the crossroads at Spottsylvania Courthouse.

We were determined to stop them even though we were outnumbered two to one. We got to the crossroads first and hastily dug more than four miles of trenches in the thick woods to block the Federal advance. We dug with bayonets, tin drinking cups, and our bare hands because we didn't have any spades. We planned to give the Yankees a warm welcome when they arrived.

The battle for Spottsylvania Courthouse began with a Federal assault against our line on May 10. Fighting raged around our regiment for two days and nights, but we were held in reserve until we were needed to repulse the advancing Yankees on May 12 at a place called the Mule Shoe. General Lee personally tried to accompany us during this fight to witness our advance, but our shouts of "Lee to the rear! Lee to the rear!" and one-armed General Gordon's persuasion caused General Lee to reconsider the wisdom of coming with us. This particular fight was very intense but lasted only half an hour.

The next morning, the Yankees attacked again and again, and each time we repulsed them even though many of our guns misfired because of the damp, foggy morning air. A heavy rain began about eight a.m., but both sides fought on and on, slipping and sliding on our earthworks which had been turned to mud by rainwater and blood. At times the fighting was hand-to-hand and a great number of men were lost on both sides.

While all this was going on, our engineers were feverishly constructing a new line of earthworks five hundred yards to the rear. In the dark early morning hours of May 13, we were notified that the new earthworks were completed, so unit by unit we took up new positions there. We were exhausted.

When dawn broke, we could see the desolation which lay before us. All the vegetation was completely shredded; even the largest trees were reduced to splinters. Corpses covered the battlefield. At the time, I estimated there were about five thousand Confederate corpses and nine thousand Union corpses, although later I learned that the actual numbers were about 1500 of our men and 2700 Yankees. We also lost about three thousand of our men who were captured, and we captured just over two thousand Yankees. My brother-in-law Rete Hicks was wounded in the thigh and sent home on wounded furlough. We had been in almost continuous rain for five days and were ready for some dry weather.

On May 19 we were back in action. We conducted a reconnaissance in force to locate the northern flank of the Union Army. In the late afternoon, we ran into a Union force and became involved in a skirmish and we were still occupied with them at nine o'clock in the evening. Because it was getting dark, General Lee ordered us to break away from this battle and return to our own lines. As we attempted to return, we got lost in the dark.

Suddenly I heard a voice: "Where do you think you're going, Reb?" followed by, "Look here, boys! We've caught ourselves a major!"

It was a Yankee infantryman. His maroon insignia told me that he and his company had recently been transferred from the artillery. I was embarrassed to find that my well-seasoned infantry soldiers had just been captured by a bunch of greenhorn Yankees who had almost no infantry experience.

The Yankees herded us into railroad boxcars along with about nine hundred other prisoners and there were 128 Yankee guards aboard also, some riding on top of the train. Our locomotive displayed two white flags which meant our train of eighteen boxcars was an "extra" and had the right-of-way over other trains. We rode in those miserable conveyances for several days and nights at speeds as great as twenty-five miles per hour, stopping only for food and water. We felt like cattle.

When we arrived at our destination, we learned we were on the shore of the Delaware Bay and we could see Fort Delaware on Pea Patch Island in the distance. The Yankees had turned the fort into a prison and we learned that it was to be our new home. It was just a short trip by steamboat ferry to the fort.

On the island, we were carefully searched for weapons and then marched under guard to our quarters. The enlisted men and junior officers were assigned to rude wooden barracks outside the main fort and given bunks stacked three high.

As I was a major, I was assigned quarters inside the masonry fort. I shared a room called a casemate with another officer. This room was well-lighted and warm, and open on one side into the large mess area where we ate at long wooden tables. The food that the Yankees provided was meager and not very good, but we officers were allowed to buy additional provisions from a free black woman who was a local resident. She also cooked for us and did our laundry, all for seven dollars per week. In addition, many people sent donations of food to the island, so our rations were really not bad at all. The men who were housed in the wooden barracks, or "bull pen," were not so fortunate; their food was poor and meager and their quarters were infested with lice, rats, and mosquitoes. Malaria, dysentery, and scurvy were rampant.

According to the *Philadelphia Inquirer* newspaper, the island contained a "population of Southern tourists who came at the urgent invitation of Mr. Lincoln."

Because of our location in the middle of the bay, escape was nearly impossible, so we were given the run of the island. We were allowed to fish in the bay and to buy additional provisions such as pickles, cheese, sardines, and pies, as well as stationery, fish hooks, shoe laces, and tobacco from the civilian merchant's store operated by local residents.

We were allowed to write letters, but they were limited to one page each in order to reduce the volume of mail.

One morning after breakfast I sat down across the table from my roommate. He was a colonel, a West Point graduate, and I thought he might answer some questions for me.

I said, "Colonel, how long do you think we're going to be kept here? What do you know that I don't know?"

The colonel said, "I don't have any inside information, but I think they're going to keep us here until the end of the war."

"What about parole?" I asked. "Don't you think they'll exchange us for some of their people?"

"John," he said, "Where have you been? Mr. Lincoln ended all the exchanges a year ago."

"What!" I exclaimed. "We've got a lot of Yankee prisoners. Doesn't he want them back?"

The Colonel said, "When we exchange prisoners, the basic idea is that we give them one of their men and they give us one of ours. That seems fair, but that's not the way Lincoln thinks. Lincoln sees this as a war of attrition. Lincoln can get all the replacements he wants, so to him, his soldiers are expendable. We need every man we can get, because we don't have many replacements. Lincoln sees the exchanges working to our advantage."

"That's pretty cold-hearted," I said. "I know Lincoln has misguided sympathy for the slaves and wants to preserve the Union, but I didn't know he cares so little for his own men."

The colonel went on. "It's worse than that, John. After Lincoln stopped the exchanges, both sides were inundated with prisoners -- more than they could handle -- that they couldn't exchange. The Yankees have the resources to house and feed thousands of Rebel soldiers, but we're struggling to supply our own troops and simply don't have the additional wherewithal to support a bunch of Yankees. That's why conditions are so bad at some of our prisons such as Andersonville down near your place and Libby Prison in Richmond. We can't help it. In fact, President Davis has asked Lincoln to resume the prisoner exchanges on humanitarian grounds, but so far Lincoln has not answered his appeals. Even worse, although the Yankees have plenty of supplies for their prisons, they have deliberately put our men on starvation rations in retaliation for the treatment their men are receiving. At least we have a good excuse; the Yankees don't. That's why the poor boys who live in those miserable barracks outside are having such a rough time. I wish we could help them somehow."

I really didn't know Lincoln was such a barbarian.

The next day, I wrote a letter to the New York *News*. I said I was in need of money and clothing. I said I owned a farm near Andersonville Prison in Georgia and if anyone with a relative imprisoned at Andersonville would send money or clothing to Fort Delaware, I would see that the relative would get similar supplies from my farm. No supplies came while I was there, but I learned that some supplies came later and were distributed to the prisoners.

One morning we had roll call especially early. When the sergeant finished calling the names, he asked, "Does anybody know where Johnson and McAllister went?"

Someone answered, "I think they got up early to go fishing while the fish are biting. They planned to come back before roll call, but you came early this morning. Are they in trouble?"

"No, they're not in trouble," said the sergeant, "but I need them back here as soon as possible."

Turning to two of the soldiers he brought with him, he ordered, "Go find those two fine Southern gentlemen and get them back here as quick as you can!"

Then he addressed the rest of us: "By nine o'clock, you will have your breakfast finished, all the tables cleared, all the dishes washed and put away, and your beds made. And no one is to leave this room. Is that understood? No one is to leave this room."

"What's going on?" someone asked.

The sergeant replied, "Can't say. All I know is, orders is orders, and all of you Southern gentlemen had better be here at nine o'clock." With that, he turned around and left, and posted guards at the doors on his way out.

Promptly at nine o'clock, a Yankee lieutenant came in and called us to attention. None of us had ever seen him before. We noticed that he walked with a slight limp, which is probably why he was assigned to Fort Delaware.

"Fall in!" he barked, and we arranged ourselves in a straight line across the room. "I'm going to call some names," he said. "If I call your name, I want you to respond 'Here, sir,' and take one step forward."

At that moment, McAllister and Johnson appeared. "Glad you could join us this morning," said the lieutenant. "Fall into line!"

Then he produced a list from his pocket and called off some names from the list. He called forty-seven of the two-hundred-odd officers in the room. Then he said, "If I did not call your name, go to your room and stay there. If I did call your name, remain where you are."

After the room was cleared of those whom he did not call, he ordered, "Dress right, dress!" and we instinctively formed a straight line, evenly spaced, and we actually looked pretty good despite our worn, shabby uniforms. On the command, "Attention," our heads snapped forward and we stood motionless like wooden soldiers, not knowing what to expect next.

Some of us had attended military schools such as Virginia Military Institute or The Citadel. They said they felt like they were back in school.

Presently, Captain Ahl came in, and we knew that something important was going on. He produced another list from his pocket. Then he said, "At ease, gentlemen," and asked each man his name and rank and checked him off his list as he went. When he came to the end of the list, he ordered, "Attention! Right face! Forward march!" and we marched in single file under guard from the fort to the dock.

"Halt!" He ordered. Then he called the roll again, and said, "All right, gentlemen, I think you can relax. Fifty prisoners -- five generals, fifteen colonels, fifteen lieutenant colonels, and fifteen majors -- will be paroled (exchanged) for a like number of Yankee officers (Actually there were only forty-seven of us). We are going to take you to Charleston, where you will be exchanged for forty-seven Union officers. You can expect at least one stop along the way. I don't want any funny business, or we'll call the whole thing off and you will be returned here to Fort Delaware. Do I make myself clear?"

"Yes, sir!" we replied in unison. None of us expected this turn of events.

We were transferred to Hilton Head, South Carolina, on June 25, 1864, aboard a prison ship called the *Dragoon* before there was a response from my letter to the *News*. I had been a prisoner of war at Fort Delaware for about six weeks.

Before we were paroled, the Yankees made us swear an oath that we would not take up arms against the United States again and that we would abide by the laws wherever we abided. The Yankees promised not to molest us so long as we lived up to our side of the agreement. We all swore to the oath, but did not feel bound by it since it was made under duress.

At ten o'clock on Tuesday morning, August 2, 1864, the *Dragoon* took us from Hilton Head to a point about a mile off Fort Sumter. The spot was marked by a buoy. As we approached under a flag of truce, we could see a Confederate vessel, the *Chesterfield*, approaching from the opposite direction. I must admit that compared to the *Dragoon*, the *Chesterfield* appeared to be a miserable, disreputable floating wreck in bad need of fresh paint and with piles of firewood for her boilers stacked on her decks. I learned she was scheduled for overhaul soon. I estimated that she could carry about twelve hundred men. Whatever her appearance, she was in good working order, and we were glad to get aboard her so we could once again be among friends. The Union officers who were being exchanged were equally glad to be among their friends. As the two ships parted to go their separate ways, we could hear the raucous celebrations aboard the *Dragoon*. Our celebrations were more subdued. We were just glad to be among Southerners again.

Each of us carried with us a certificate that we had taken the oath. As soon as we were safely aboard the *Chesterfield* and out of sight of the *Dragoon*, we tore our certificates into shreds as a symbol of our contempt. We became known as the "Immortal Fifty," not to be confused with a more famous group of officers known as the "Immortal Six Hundred" who were used as human shields.

C h a p t e r   I X

More from Pa

One morning I was in Oglethorpe on business when I saw Sam Talbot across the street at the bank. I walked over to speak to him, and he said, "Joe, I'm glad to see you. I've got something I want to ask you about. Have you got a minute? Come into my office."

I sat down across the desk from Sam. We talked about the weather. He asked me about Mary and all the kids, and then he said, "I know it's none of my business, Joe, but I want to ask you about your cotton. Have you sold last year's crop?"

"I wish I could sell it, but with those damn Yankees blockading our ports, I can't sell it. There's no market a-tall, and if I could sell it right now, I couldn't get much for it because the market is so depressed. I really don't know what I'm going to do, and I hear all the other planters are in the same fix."

"How much do you have, Joe?" asked Sam.

I replied, "I don't know exactly, but the big barn is full up to the rafters, so I figure it must be somewhere near one-and-a-half million pounds. You know it takes roughly three pounds of seed cotton to make one pound of lint cotton, so that's 500,000 pounds of lint cotton. At five hundred pounds per bale, that's about a thousand bales after it's ginned and baled. With the market busted, I didn't want to spend the money it takes to gin it, so I just piled it up in the barn. Why do you ask?"

Sam said, "Would you be willing to take two cents per pound for it as is with the seeds still in it?"

I said, "Sam, what on earth are you going to do with a thousand bales of raw cotton? And don't you know that's nowhere near a fair price? That's only six cents a pound for the fiber after the seeds are removed since the seeds are two thirds of the weight but have very little value."

"I think I have a market for it," Sam said. "How sure are you about that thousand bales?"

I said, "Well, I've had that barn for several years now, and I have a pretty good idea about what it'll hold. I could be off a little."

Sam said, "That's all right, I'll take your word for it. If you'll take two cents per pound, as is, I can have you a check for thirty thousand dollars in two weeks. We won't need to weigh it now, but I might need you to weigh it for me when I come for it. You'll have to keep it in your barn until I need it, and I'll haul it out of there when the time comes. It may be two or three years."

"Wait a minute, Sam," I said. "I really need to use my barn, so if it's going to stay full of cotton for a couple of years, I'll need five hundred dollars a year to store it for you."

"That's fair," said Sam. "Thirty thousand dollars in two weeks, with another five hundred dollars at the end of next year?"

"Just a minute," I said. "Tell me about the rest of this deal. I know you don't have a need for a thousand bales of cotton. What are you going to do with it?"

So Sam explained. "The Confederate Government has a program called Produce Loans. They'll lend me the money, as much as I need, to buy cotton, so I'll be able to pay you as soon as I get the money from the Government. In turn, I'll sell the cotton to the Government, and they've guaranteed to pay me and some other bankers a certain fixed price when the war is over so we can repay the loans and make some money to boot. The Government will ship the cotton by train to the Rio Grande River in Texas, where Mexican speculators will pay our Government for it and export it from Mexico to England, and some will go to France and Russia, too. That's how we'll get around that damned blockade. The Government will use the money they get from the speculators to buy rifles, canons, and other European war materiel and raw materials such as sulfur, copper, and saltpeter from the Mexicans, so you see, I can make a little money, you can a make a little money, and we can help the Confederacy with the war all at the same time. And the best part is, we do it all with money we borrow from the Government, so we have absolutely no risk at all."

"Damn!" I said. "No wonder bankers all get rich!" and we shook hands.

In actual practice, cotton producers in Texas were able to supply most of the cotton needed by the Mexicans. Although Sam paid me for my cotton and resold it to the Confederate Government, no one ever came to get it. When the Confederacy collapsed, the cotton was still in my barn, so after the war, I was able to sell the same cotton to my cousin Isaac who had a cotton gin and warehouse in Reynolds. He had lost his warehouse and all his cotton in a fire, and was in dire need of seed cotton to replace his inventory and keep his gin running.

The sale of this cotton to Isaac worked out really well for me. Isaac and I both knew of a certain farm that would soon be coming up for sale in a public auction and we both planned to bid on it. But after he bought my cotton, I had enough cash so that I easily outbid him at the auction. In a sense, I outbid Isaac with his own money.

Chapter   X

Joe Jr

I resumed my duties with the army in Lynchburg after my furlough in Georgia. I told my Captain, "Lieutenant Joe Carson Jr. reporting for duty."

The city of Lynchburg was a major transportation center located on the James River, the Kanawha Canal, and three railroads. It was blessed with public water and sewer systems, a gas works for lighting, and telegraph service to Richmond. It depended upon the manufacture of tobacco products, especially chewing tobacco, for its livelihood. However, unlike factories in the North, the tobacco factories were not mechanized but depended upon hand labor, mostly performed by slaves.

The population in 1860 was about 6800 souls, the sixth-largest city in Virginia, and in terms of per-capita income it was the second-wealthiest city in the (former) United States second only to New Bedford, Massachusetts. The citizens of Lynchburg were decidedly pro-Union because they feared the loss of their Northern markets if Virginia seceded. However, after Virginia joined the Confederacy, most of the citizens became loyal Confederates and many Lynchburg men joined the Confederate army.

In the summer of 1864, the Yanks had General Lee bottled up in Petersburg. The Yankees tried to destroy Lynchburg's canal and railroads but were defeated and fled to safety all the way to West Virginia.

This Union defeat at Lynchburg left the Shenandoah Valley largely unprotected and General Lee sensed an opportunity. Lee sent General Jubal Early with a force of fifteen thousand men to move northward up the Shenandoah, then swing around and attack Washington, D. C. from the north, hopefully drawing some of Grant's Federal forces away from Petersburg.

On the morning of July 9, we met the Yanks on the banks of the Monocacy River just south of Frederick, Maryland. They had been warned of our presence in the area and had hastily assembled a defense force of some 6500 frightened Union reservists.

Our division, commanded by General John B. Gordon, was ordered to attack about three o'clock in the afternoon. Our advance was hindered by a number of stout fences that we had to climb over. The Yanks managed to kill or wound several of our officers very quickly and General Gordon's horse was also killed, so we were thrown into disarray. We were able to get reorganized within an hour or so, but this gave the Yanks just enough time to take up strong defensive positions behind rock walls and fences and across the Monocacy River on the east bank's higher ground. Other Confederate divisions had a little more success, but slowly, so that at nightfall we were obliged to set up camp on the battlefield within two days' march of Washington. We could see the Federal Capitol's new dome with our telescopes. During the night, the Federals were able to bring up reinforcements, so in the morning we abandoned the attack and returned to Virginia. This was the Confederacy's last foray into the North. Following the Battle of the Monocacy, all our battles were fought on Southern ground.

By early March of 1865, our situation in Richmond and Petersburg was becoming desperate. General Lee had fifty thousand seasoned veterans under his command, a formidable army, but we were surrounded on three sides by more than 200,000 Federal troops under the command of General Grant. Our lines were stretched thinner and thinner as the Yankees extended the siege. In addition, Union General Sherman and his army of Federal arsonists and vandals had completed their infamous march through Georgia and had now turned toward Richmond. Confederate General Johnston had been unable to stop them at Bentonville, North Carolina, in March, 1865.

When the Yankees captured the Richmond and Danville Railroad, the last rail line into Petersburg, General Lee saw that the South's last hope lay in our army's escape from Richmond and Petersburg. He gave the task of plotting this escape to General John B. Gordon.

After thorough personal reconnaissance to find the weakest spot in the enemy lines, Gordon devised a plan and presented it to Lee, who approved it on March 23, 1865.

I had been elected captain in 1863. Pursuant to Gordon's plan, I was placed in command of a hundred hand-picked sharpshooters, the best that could be found on short notice. The men were armed with Whitworth rifles, which fired unusual hexagonal bullets for extra range and accuracy. Under cover of darkness in the wee hours of the morning, I assembled my men opposite a Yankee fortification called Fort Stedman.

I noticed my younger brother Bob in the group. I knew Pa had corresponded with General Philip Cook and received assurances that Bob could be a courier which would keep him away from the fighting, so Pa had reluctantly given Bob permission to join the army. Bob had joined the Twelfth Georgia Regiment on April 1, 1864, one day before his eighteenth birthday, but had soon transferred to my regiment, the Fourth Georgia, and was serving as a courier for General Cook. I was surprised to see Bob among my men. I said, "Bob, what are you doing here?"

Bob said, "I heard you were leading this attack and I want to go along. I want to be there for you in case you are hurt. General Cook said I could come."

Who was I to countermand the general? I said, "All right, then, come along. Here, take my jacket, this night air is a little chilly. Keep your head down."

General Gordon himself came to give us a pep talk in hushed tones. One of our men must have made a little noise, because through the darkness came the voice of a Yankee picket. "What's going on over there, Reb?"

Gordon was petrified, but one of our quick-thinking pickets replied, "We're just gathering a little firewood. Go back to sleep, Yank!"

Gordon finished his talk and signaled our picket to fire his gun, the pre-arranged signal for our attack to begin. Our picket and the

Yankee picket had become friends when they weren't shooting at each other, so our picket shouted, "Look out, Yank! Here we come!" and fired his gun.

First, special squads of our men cleared avenues through our own defenses so our soldiers could get into the no-man's land between the lines. Next, fifty men with axes cleared a pathway through the Federal defenses, which consisted of a ring of brush piled up around the fort, and beyond that, a ring of fraises (a medieval defensive device also called "cheval de frise") with plenty of sharp spikes and tied together with wire. Then, I and my hundred sharpshooters rushed through the opening and attacked Fort Stedman itself.

The fort was situated on a little rise and consisted of a palisade of sharpened logs surrounded by a moat. Five hundred Yankee soldiers attempted to defend the fort, but they had difficulty seeing us in the darkness. Whenever one of them raised his head above the palisade to aim, our sharpshooters were able to pick him off. As a result, many of the Yankees simply held their rifles above the palisade and fired without aiming.

Somehow, we were able to capture Fort Stedman along with eight cannon, numerous rifles, and the entire garrison of men and officers. It was not until the battle was over that I discovered my brother Bob lying dead in the no-man's land between the two opposing lines. His body was still wearing the jacket that I had lent him.

According to Gordon's plan, two other companies of sharpshooters led by local guides were to capture two more forts behind the enemy lines, thus clearing a pathway for Gordon's entire force of fifteen thousand men to rush through and disrupt Yankee communications and generally cause havoc. With good fortune, they might even have captured Grant's headquarters. However, in the darkness and confusion, they failed to reach their objectives so the attack failed except for our victory at Fort Stedman.

The next morning, the Yankees advanced with superior forces and we were forced to withdraw. I carried Bob's body back to our lines across my shoulders, and it was struck twice by the hail of bullets that followed us. This probably saved my life for I surely would have been killed if it were not for Bob's body across my shoulders. I was forced to bury my brother near our camp, but when the war was over I removed it and re-buried it behind Pa's house near our mother and our brother James.

General Gordon was wounded – again – at Fort Stedman. My horse was shot through the nose, but survived, and is still serving me.

General Gordon's plan failed, but in a sense it succeeded. The Yankees moved some of their forces to strengthen the area around Fort Stedman. This left another part of the Yankee line in a weakened condition, and General Lee and his army were able to escape through that point. But, it was too late. Lee surrendered at Appomattox Courthouse on April 9, 1865.

When the Confederate Army abandoned its defensive positions around Richmond, word quickly spread among the civilian population and pandemonium ensued. Confederate bureaucrats hastily burned uncirculated Confederate money and their important documents on the sidewalks in front of their buildings. The embers from these burnings set fire to the downtown commercial district of Richmond. Civilian residents and shopkeepers of the downtown area gathered on the lush green grass of Capitol Square and watched with shock and dismay as their homes and businesses were consumed by the flames and Confederate arsenals exploded. When Federal troops entered the city, one of their first tasks was to assist the local fire department in extinguishing the blazes, otherwise the whole city might have been lost. Many of the citizens of Richmond said the Yankees had started the fire. When it was all over, fifty-four city blocks had been burned. The Federal soldiers also had to disperse several mobs that were looting some of the stores.

Years later, General Gordon said this concerning Fort Stedman: "Why did we fail? I'll tell you why. God did not intend that we should succeed. He did not intend that the Southern Confederacy should be an accomplished fact. He was in command."

John Thomas

After I was paroled from Fort Delaware, I made a quick visit home to see how Saphronia, Pa, and everybody were getting along. I was pleased and proud to find that Saphronia was keeping our farm running very well with only a little help and advice from Pa. Melissa was becoming a shrewd business woman. Charlotte, whom I hired as a tutor, was doing an excellent job with the children, teaching them things like table manners and Bible stories in addition to their ABC's.

The arithmetic book that Charlotte used asked the question, "If one Confederate soldier can whip seven Yankees, how many soldiers can whip 49 Yanks?" This book was produced in wartime haste and contained a number of errors in English grammar and style, but Charlotte was grateful for any kind of arithmetic book.

I could only hope that someday my children could be proud that their father, John Thomas Carson, had played a part in preserving the freedom of the Confederate States of America.

Saphronia said wartime shortages were becoming a nuisance, but they had not yet become a real hardship for our family. Of course, most manufactured goods, especially cloth and many food items, were in short supply because most of them came from up north or were imported and what little cloth was produced in Southern mills was used for uniforms. Homespun dresses for the ladies became fashionable as a symbol of Southern patriotism. Cast iron goods were hard to get because the foundries in Macon, Birmingham, and Atlanta had all diverted their production to war material. Many Southern governors, including our own Governor Brown, begged farmers to produce less cotton and more food, and Pa and Saphronia decided to plant extra corn, peas, and wheat during the war years. These crops looked strange in fields that were usually full of cotton.

Some families could not afford Christmas presents for their children during the war. The children were told not to expect Christmas presents because the Yankees had shot Santa Claus.

Cotton cards (wire brushes with very short, stiff bristles and wooden backs) used in processing raw cotton into thread, were also in short supply. The state government supplied them free of charge to indigent families.

Many Southern ladies knitted socks or sewed shirts and pants and sent them to the army where they were gratefully received.

Pa said the worst shortage was salt. The war had severely disrupted our supply of salt, and without salt we had no means of preserving meat. The government instituted a rationing system under which certain eligible families were able to buy limited quantities of salt from the State of Georgia for one dollar per half bushel, while the price on the open market soared to twenty-four dollars per half bushel. Some families resorted to recovering salt from the floors of their smoke houses.

The falling value of Confederate currency caused prices to inflate. A pound of butter cost twelve cents in 1861, but by 1865 it was five dollars. A bushel of corn rose from two dollars to fourteen dollars, and other prices rose by similar amounts. Many people and businesses were forced to resort to bartering.

Since my oath was null and void, I soon returned to my army duties under General Gordon in the Shenandoah Valley. Presently I found myself in the heat of battle at Winchester, Virginia -- a prosperous commercial center of 4400 people -- on September 19, 1864, where I was struck by enemy bullets three times. I was taken by ambulance to the rail depot and then by train to Hospital No. 3 in Lynchburg. In the ambulance I told the chaplain, "Brother Brooks, I have tried to do my duty as a soldier of my country, and in an humble, hobbling way, I have tried to follow Jesus....Blessed be His holy name."

I was surprised to find Joe in the same ward with me. Joe had been wounded in the same battle but I was so weak and so full of morphine that I really didn't talk to him very much.

Dock and Mose found us in the hospital and are doing what they can for us. Please tell Saphronia that I love her. I fear I will not survive these wounds.

Chapter XII

Joe Jr.

John Thomas died of gangrene on September 30, 1864. I was still in the hospital recovering from my wounds when he passed away and I was able to write his obituary from my hospital bed. I wrote, "He was a man of strong character, a brave and efficient officer, an earnest and enthusiastic Confederate having implicit faith in the justness of our cause. He was kind and courteous to all with whom he came in contact and was beloved by his comrades. In his death the Twelfth Georgia Regiment lost one of its best and bravest officers."

The ladies of Lynchburg under the leadership of Mrs. Lucy Otey organized themselves into the Ladies Relief Society and made bandages and uniforms for the many army hospitals in Lynchburg. One day, some ladies brought gingerbread with raisin sauce for every man in the ward. One of the ladies handed me a bowl and said, "This will help you get better. It's man food. I hope you like it. I made it myself and Mary Alice over there made the sauce."

Taking a bite, I said, "Oh yes ma'am, it's real good. Thank you." And then as an afterthought, I asked, "Do you happen to know a girl named Charlotte Briggs? She's from right here in Lynchburg."

She answered, "Why yes, I think I do know her, but I haven't seen her in some time now. A beautiful girl, educated at Mr. Brown's Female Academy. Her father's a preacher. Reverend Briggs was just ready to retire when the war came, but he wanted to do his part, so he stayed on at his church so some other, younger preacher could become a chaplain in the army. It's been quite difficult for Reverend Briggs, what with all the mothers and widows needing comfort and reassurance. Do you know her?"

"Yes," I replied. "My brother hired her as a tutor for his children and I escorted her to Georgia for him. Just before I left home to come back to my unit, we became engaged and she's going to be Mrs. Joseph Perryman Carson if I ever get out of this hospital bed."

"Good for you, young man," said the gingerbread lady. "I'm sure you'll make a handsome couple."

And with that, she picked up my empty bowl and walked away.

Chapter XIII

Pa Remembers the Burial of John Thomas 1864

M any Georgia families could not afford to bring their deceased loved ones home. But when we received the letter from Joe telling us of John Thomas' death, Saphronia and her eldest son Albert set off in their wagon to fetch his body home for burial. But they hadn't got very far when they met Mose bringing his body home in another wagon. We buried John Thomas in his metal coffin (railroads required metal coffins when shipping corpses long distances, especially in hot weather) near his mother and his brother James behind my house. He had a Masonic funeral. We marked his grave with a wooden cross, and after the war we replaced the wooden cross with a tall obelisk bearing an image of his sword. May he rest in peace.

Chapter XIV

Joe Jr.'s Memories of a Conscientious Objector and More Hospitals 1865

O ne of my first assignments after my release from the hospital was to sit on a court-martial. The most interesting case we heard that day concerned a man who had refused an order to fight. We asked him why. He said, "I'm a Quaker, and the Holy Bible forbids us to kill. We're under the command of our God, our Lord Jesus Christ, and the Still Small Voice. Thou committeth a grievous sin if thou takest a life. Thou must not kill, but turn thine other cheek to thine enemies."

"What is this Still Small Voice?" we asked.

"Doth thou not know? He is the The Holy Spirit, the Counselor who teacheth us to tell good from evil and comforteth us in the night," he replied.

"Does your religion prevent you from all military duty, or just fighting?" we asked.

"Most of the brethren and sistren in our meeting say that all military service is wrong," he said. "I used to feel that way too, but since the Yankees have occupied my farm and turned all that I own to the Devil's work, I decided to join the effort to drive them back to their own homes. I don't hate them nor wish them any harm, but I pray that the forces of evil will soon leave this valley. I've seen them up close and I know what they are. I will not smite them, but I pray the Lord will smite them and my soul will not be judged guilty."

He talked funny, but we were impressed by his sincerity. Since the army needed all the able-bodied men we could muster, we did not discharge him from the army nor send him to the stockade, but assigned him to non-combat duty. The regiment was ordered to Petersburg a few days later, and the court-martial never met again.

During our army's escape from Petersburg on Monday, April 3, 1865, I was wounded again and taken to Receiving and Wayside Hospital Number Nine which was housed in an old tobacco warehouse near the river in Richmond. This warehouse was always papered with advertising posters for shows, circuses, politicians and the like, and was known as "The Billboard of Richmond." It occupied almost an entire city block. As a hospital, it had more than nine hundred beds and 150 employees.

Joseph Mayo, the mayor of Richmond, surrendered the city to the Yankees on the same day that I was taken to the hospital, and Richmond, including the hospital with all the staff and patients, was overrun by Yankees. I remained at Hospital Number Nine until I was transferred to Stuart Hospital, also in Richmond.

Stuart Hospital was set up in sixteen old buildings that once were the barracks of the city guard at the old fairgrounds. The hospital had about five hundred patients from both armies, and as far as I could tell, the staff treated us all equally well as best they could. The hospital was crawling with Union guards and they gave the doctors and nurses a difficult time. Then one day, I overheard the chief surgeon, Dr. Palmer, pigeon-hole the Yankee captain in the hallway and complain about the treatment his staff received from the guards. He said, "Look here, Captain. This is a hospital. We're doing the best we can for these men under difficult circumstances. We're overloaded, short-handed, and low on supplies, and your men aren't making it any easier. We've always treated anybody who came in, no matter what color his uniform, and we don't intend to stop now. Most of these brave men are too sick to do any harm, so I don't expect they can give you any trouble, and if they do it'll be my responsibility, not yours. Besides, the war is over. Why don't you and your men ease off?"

After that, things seemed to get better.

The Yankees wanted Stuart Hospital for their own sick and wounded soldiers, and as I wasn't strong enough to make the journey home, I was sent to Jackson Hospital by ambulance because that's where most of the sick and wounded boys from Georgia were.

After I began to feel better, I had the opportunity to talk to some of the other patients. Many of them were amputees and most of them said they felt no pain during their operations thanks to the use of chloroform and ether. They had plenty of pain after the drugs wore off, but it was worthwhile, because without the surgery they might have died of gangrene and blood poisoning.

One of the surgeons told me, "Surgeons are often accused of performing too many amputations, but actually we don't perform enough, and many patients die who could be saved. Amputations are not possible for patients who are wounded in the chest or abdomen, so in those cases, all we can do is to keep them comfortable with morphine -- and pray for them."

A large number of our boys had accepted Christ during their time in the army, and Baptist, Methodist, and Presbyterian preachers conducted services in the hospital for us on Sundays.

I remained in Jackson Hospital, more like a prisoner than a patient, until the end of May. Jackson Hospital had a forty-acre garden that supplied vegetables for the patients, and I was assigned to tend it along with several other convalescing patients.

While I was still in Jackson Hospital, I learned that only one hundred of the original thousand or so officers and men who enlisted in our Fourth Georgia Regiment in 1861 surrendered at Appomattox in 1865, and only sixty-five of the original thousand in John Thomas' Twelfth Georgia Regiment were left to surrender at Appomattox.

By the end of May, I had regained enough strength to travel and I was eager to see Charlotte and Pa. Lincoln's successor, Andrew Johnson, issued an Amnesty Proclamation and under its terms, I was allowed to take the Amnesty Oath and go home. I was not really surprised to find Dock and Mose already at home when I arrived. They remained in our employ during the remainder of their lives and became more like close family friends and we took care of them in their old age.

All three of the hospitals where I was in Richmond were very clean, well-ventilated, and situated in pleasant residential areas of the city. Despite the seriousness of their wounds, seventy-five per cent of the amputees at Confederate hospitals in Richmond and Lynchburg survived. In this regard, the record of these hospitals was better than almost any other hospitals in the world.

Chapter   X V

Pa Recollects

During April, 1865, a Union cavalry force called Wilson's Raiders swept across west-central Georgia from Columbus to Macon (which they captured without resistance on April 20, 1865), and then south to Reynolds and down the River Road into Macon County, raiding supplies as they went. They camped at several of the Flint River crossings in an attempt to intercept Jefferson Davis, who was fleeing from Federal authorities. We knew the Raiders were coming, so we hid our silver and other valuables in the swamp.

My daughter Mary Jane and I were sitting on my porch when a Yankee soldier rode up to us and demanded to know where our valuables were and if we had seen two strangers driving a buggy and heading south. They threatened to kill us if we refused to tell them where our valuables were. I said, "If you kill me, you will not rob me of many years."

We said we had not seen any strangers, which was the truth. Mary Jane thought her Pa was very brave to stand up to those armed men, but I knew that what I had done was nothing compared to what her brothers had done in the army.

The soldiers searched the house and barns but did not molest us further, and took only my favorite horse and all of the chickens.

The Yankees used the Miona Springs Hotel as a base while they thoroughly searched our area. While the Yankees were lurking about, James' widow Melissa sat up every night with a shotgun to protect her family, but the Yankees never went near her farm.

Men from the First Wisconsin and Fourth Michigan Calvary did capture President and Mrs. Davis and their children near Irwinville, Georgia, before dawn on May 10, 1865. Davis was coming down with a cold and when he was captured he was wearing a shawl Mrs. Davis had given him to protect him from the cool early morning air. Yankee newspapers ridiculed Davis, saying that he was disguised as a woman when captured, some even picturing him wearing a hoop skirt. The Yankees especially reviled Davis because they (mistakenly) believed he was complicit in the assassination of Abraham Lincoln.

Davis and his family and a few loyal advisors were camped in the woods on the edge of a swamp with less than a hundred Confederate soldiers and sailors who acted as guards for the presidential entourage. The men from Michigan and Wisconsin approached the camp from two different directions and in the darkness, they mistook each other for Davis' Confederate guards and began firing at each other. Two Yankees were killed and four were wounded. No members of Davis' party were injured -- in fact, none of them even fired a shot.

Some newspapers said after Atlanta fell to Union forces under General Sherman, the Confederate Army destroyed the rail line from Atlanta to Chattanooga, but it was actually the Yankees who destroyed it so that the Confederate army could not attack them from the rear. This cut the Yankee supply line. Sherman decided to march his army to Savannah, foraging for supplies as he went. He did not want to abandon Atlanta to the Confederate Army, so he ordered all five thousand Atlanta citizens to evacuate the city and burned everything that might have any military usefulness.

Sherman's march through Georgia cut our state in half, but his forces stayed north of our area. The only Yankees we saw were that one escapee I encountered at the ferry and those pilfering rascals from Wilson's Raiders. Otherwise, our area survived the war without physical damage.

Things were different in Milledgeville, the state capitol. The Yankees burned the penitentiary, the Oconee River Bridge, the depot, and the state arsenal and powder magazine. They held a mock session of the legislature during which they repealed the Ordinance of Secession. They ransacked the statehouse, and even desecrated the state chapel by housing cavalry horses in the chapel and pouring honey and molasses down the pipes of the organ. What sort of men were these who would desecrate the house of God?

One morning the slaves – former slaves, that is -- came to my back door. They said, "Master Joe, we done had us a meetin'. We knows we is free and we can go anywheres we wants, but dis plantation is our home and we don't want to go nowheres else. Besides, where would we go? Dis plantation and workin' for you is all we knows, so if it be's all right with you, we'll jes' stay on at dis place and we'll keep on workin' together jes' like we done before. We knows you'll treat us right."

I agreed. I knew that I would continue to be responsible for their food, clothing, shelter, and medical care for serious illnesses. For minor illnesses, the slaves had a surprising repertoire of effective home remedies and I even used them once or twice myself. I agreed to pay the former slaves a small wage for their work, but I was really grateful for their loyalty. I suppose our kindness toward them over the years had paid off.

Many of them asked to take "Carson" as their last name. I was honored.

I will readily admit that things were different on many plantations. In some places the slaves erupted into wild celebrations of their new freedom and soon set off to seek their fortunes in a new and exciting world of opportunity only to come back home to beg for their old jobs, having found that making a living away from their home plantations was much more difficult than they expected. Of course, their former masters were glad to have them back, because they needed the labor to run their farms.

Later that day I thought about what I had lost during the war. I had lost my Martha and three of my sons, John Thomas, James, and Bob. But I had gained a new wife, Mary, and a beautiful daughter-in-law, Charlotte. I still had my house and my land. The hands were staying on, so I hadn't really lost them, either.

Neither Mary nor I had ever been to Florida, so after things settled down following the war, she and I decided to make a train trip to Kissimmee. One evening after supper as we were enjoying the rocking chairs on the hotel front porch, a stranger came up to us and said, "Excuse me, sir. Do you have a farm up in Georgia near Marshallville?"

I replied, "Yes sir, I do. Why do you ask?"

The stranger continued, "Did you and a black man take a buggy across the river on a ferry one day during the war?"

Again I answered in the affirmative.

He asked, "Do you remember an encounter with a Union soldier on the road to the ferry?"

"Yes," I said, "I remember it well."

"Well, I'm that Union soldier," said the stranger. "You took me to the constable at Marshallville, who sent me back to Andersonville, and I remained there until the end of the war. Now I live here in Kissimmee."

Mary and I remarked, "It's a small world."

Chapter   X V I

Joe Jr. Remembers Reconstruction, Death of Pa, Shopping in Macon, and Volunteering at the Courthouse 1865 - 1875

Beginning in 1865, Georgia endured what the Yankees called "Reconstruction." We got a new state constitution ram-rodded through the State Convention by its anti-secessionist chairman, Herschel Johnson. In November, 1865, we elected a new governor, congressmen, and state legislators. Most Southerners expected the newly-freed former slaves to have the same limited rights that "free persons of color" had before the war, so the legislators easily ratified the Thirteenth Amendment to the United States Constitution, which ended slavery. The war was over, the Union had been preserved, and the slaves had been freed. Therefore, the army returned control of the state government to local elected officials, and Reconstruction was over. Or was it?

The legislators also selected two new United States Senators, but Congress in Washington refused to seat our new Senators and our new Congressmen.

In 1866, Congress proposed the Fourteenth Constitutional Amendment which extended citizenship to the former slaves. The Georgia Legislature ratified the Amendment in 1868.

In September, 1868, the Georgia Legislature expelled all thirty-two of its black delegates on the grounds that the State Constitution did not allow Negroes to hold public office. Later that same month there was a confrontation at a Negro Republican rally in Camilla, Georgia, in support of the Negro delegates. The confrontation resulted in the deaths of twelve Negroes and the slight injuries of seven whites. Furthermore, in the election of 1868, Georgia became one of only two Southern states to vote against Ulysses S. Grant for president. In 1869, the legislature voted against the unpopular, outlandish Fifteenth Amendment which gave former slaves the right to vote. Congress once again refused to seat the representatives from Georgia.

Because of all this, military rule across the State of Georgia resumed in December of 1869.

In January, 1870, Georgia's military governor, Alfred H. Terry, expelled all of the former Confederates from the legislature. Then he re-installed all of the Negro delegates who had been previously expelled, which created a heavy Republican majority in the legislature. In February, the newly-constituted legislature ratified the Fifteenth Amendment. In July, 1870, Georgia was readmitted to the Union and Reconstruction was over at last.

It didn't take long for carpetbaggers, opportunist scallywags, and a Federal agency called the Freedmen's Bureau to descend upon the South at the war's end and fill the former slaves' heads with all sorts of ideas. Some of my neighbors who had mistreated their slaves feared a mass uprising of the blacks and joined a secret organization called the Ku Klux Klan in order to defend their lives, property, and especially their political power. My neighbors said, "Joe Jr., why won't you and your Pa join the Klan?"

I said, "Pa and I have always had good relations with our slaves, and we want no part of the Klan's terror, beatings, and murder. We don't anticipate any trouble with our slaves," so we refused to join.

Like most Southerners, we felt that all these political machinations were Northern meddling in state business, and we were resentful. It is my personal opinion that many of the later problems between blacks and whites were caused by Reconstruction, not by the war itself.

Pa and I stood aside and watched the political upheaval with dismay, but none of it made a great difference on the plantation. The rhythm of life continued much like it had before the war.

Usually things in our part of Georgia went smoothly after the war, but not always. One Sunday morning, we arrived at church to find the front pews filled with black people. When Pa arrived, he took one look at the former slaves and said, "Get to the back of the church where you belong, you black rascals!" And they got.

Not long afterward, the white members of the congregation presented themselves as a body to the Church of Christ at Reynolds for membership and were accepted. We gave our old church building to the black congregation. This new, segregated arrangement was agreeable to both blacks and whites. The blacks, especially, welcomed the opportunity to worship as they pleased without white supervision. They wanted to hear some "real preachin'" instead of what their black preachers were told to say by their white masters.

One day a former slave girl named Charlotte Raines attempted to set fire to my house. I caught her in the act and gave her a sound thrashing with my silver-headed walking stick. She reported my "assault" to the Freedmen's Bureau, who arrested me, tried me, convicted me and sentenced me to the Federal Prison in Atlanta. On the way to prison, I encountered a carpetbagger who said he could have me set free for a three hundred dollar bribe, no questions asked. I paid him the money and was back in my own home in three days.

Pa died on April 23, 1875 at the home of his son-in-law Henry Terrell Jordan. We buried Pa behind his house near three of his sons and his beloved Martha. Mary, my step mother, moved back to Marshallville to be near her own family.

Every Spring, farmers borrowed money to purchase seeds, fertilizer, and other supplies, and repaid the loans after the harvest in the Fall. Before the war, the slaves were considered property and they were frequently used as collateral for bank loans. As free citizens they could no longer be pledged as collateral, and without collateral it became difficult for farmers to borrow the money they needed. Also, when the slaves were freed, two thirds of Macon County's tax base disappeared, and the total loss in Georgia's tax base caused by the loss of slaves as property was $454,000,000. Additionally, there was a severe drought in 1865. All of this sent the economy into a steep decline.

I was forced to use my land as collateral, but because of poor yields and low prices for cotton, by 1877 I was adjudged bankrupt and the bank, which was owned by Yankees, foreclosed on my farm. It was sold at public auction on the courthouse steps. Nobody in the area had much money, so I was able to buy it back for $181. I think I got the best of that Yankee bank because the farm was really worth much more.

I had saved my farm, but I still didn't have enough cash to pay my hands for a whole year so I resorted to the sharecropping system. In this system, I provided the land and equipment (including mules) and half of the seed and fertilizer, the hands provided all of the labor and the other half of the seed and fertilizer, and we shared the proceeds of the crops after the harvest. This system reduced my need for cash. Under sharecropping, the hands shared the risk with me and had an incentive to work harder than they had before. The hands could buy necessary supplies on credit (typically at fifteen per cent interest for six months) at a country store to get through the growing season, so I no longer had to be their banker.

Sometimes, Charlotte, Melissa and Saphronia went shopping in Macon. They left early in the morning in the buggy. Usually they took Melissa's son Charlie with them as chaperone. Charlie drove them to the depot in Reynolds and left the horse and buggy at the livery stable. They took the early morning train into Macon. The ladies spent several hours shopping for hats, fancy dresses, shoes, and other luxury items that were unavailable in rural areas. Young Charlie was fascinated by the sounds of the city, especially the cry of the newspaper boy hawking his wares: "Macon Daily Telegram! 'Lanta Constitution!"

They spent the night at Macon's Lanier Hotel, where they enjoyed a nice dinner before retiring. The next day, after breakfast, they shopped some more before catching the afternoon train back to Reynolds and Charlie redeemed the horse and buggy from the stable. They all came home loaded with boxes and bags and arrived home tired but happy.

Eventually I gave my land to my children and grandchildren, partly because I wanted to protect it from any creditors I might have in the future, but also because I was ready to retire from farming. Charlotte and I moved to a house in Reynolds.

I became interested in local politics, and often volunteered at the courthouse to register people to vote. One day a young man came to register, so I began asking him the usual questions and filling out the required form. I asked him his name, his age, and where he lived. Then I asked, "Are you a United States citizen?"

"Yes," he replied.

"Born in the United States of America?" I asked.

"No."

Looking up from the form, I said, "Oh, so you're a naturalized citizen?"

Again he answered, "No."

I put down my pen. I said, "I don't understand. If you were not born in the United States and you're not naturalized, how can you be a citizen?"

He drew himself up to his full height and said proudly, "Sir, I was born in the Confederate States of America!"

Conclusion

What are we to make of this? What conclusions can we draw?

I won't try to tell you that mistreatment of the slaves did not exist, because it did, but it was less common than many readers may believe. Masters and their slaves depended on each other, and their relationship was usually amicable. Sometimes master and slave became close personal friends. Even when master and slave were not close friends, why would someone mistreat his most valuable possessions? Out-and-out cruelty towards the slaves simply didn't make sense.

The northern abolitionists backed the South into a corner and the South came out swinging against an enemy they knew, or should have known, had more resources and was much more powerful. Southerners felt they had no choice.

Against the odds, Confederate soldiers fought honorably and well for what they believed to be right and true and we can be proud of them because they stood up for their beliefs. The Confederacy did not run out of arms and ammunition. The Confederacy simply ran out of soldiers.

Surely this great United States of America will never experience another War Between the States. Surely all Americans can recite the Pledge of Allegiance with pride. Surely all Americans can salute when Old Glory passes by in a parade and we can stand at attention when we hear the *Star Spangled Banner.*

Nevertheless, we Southerners can also take pride in our Southern heritage, and we can say with a smile, "Save your Confederate money! The South will rise again!"

Epilogue – Tying Up Loose Ends

All of the places in this story are real.

All of the characters in this story are real except the following:

- Chapter I: Aunt Bessie is a fictional character, but it may be assumed that the Carsons really did have a servant who worked as a cook at the inn.
- Chapter I: The Carsons really did have an elderly slave who sat on the porch and listened for the stage coach, but "Uncle Lucas" is a fictional name. His real name is unknown.
- Chapter VI: The messenger at Lieutenant Carson's tent is fictional, as are the sentry at John Thomas' tent and the conductor on the train from Chattanooga to Atlanta.
- Chapter VIII: The Yankee infantryman who captured John Thomas is fictional.
- Chapter VIII: At Fort Delaware, John Thomas' roommate, the colonel, is fictional, along with McAllister, Johnson, the sergeant, and the lieutenant. Captain Ahl was a real person.
- Chapter IX: Sam Talbot is fictional, but the Produce Loans Program was a real program of the Confederate Government. There's no evidence that the Carsons participated in that program. Cousin Isaac is fictional.
- Chapter XII: Mary Alice and the Gingerbread Lady are fictional.
- Chapter XIV: The Yankee captain at the hospital is fictional, and while Dr. Palmer was a real person, he may not have been in charge of the hospital after the Yankees took over.

- Chapter XVI: The Macon newspaper boy is fictional. So is the young man who registered to vote, and the story about registering to vote is a fabrication.

Most of the dialogue is the product of literary license.

The inn at Knoxville was destroyed by fire in 1924. The town of Knoxville has almost dried up, and its charter was rescinded by the Georgia General Assembly in 1995. There are just a few houses still there and the old courthouse has become a museum. Although Knoxville is no longer a town, Crawford County has a new modern courthouse within sight of the old courthouse.

The Miona Springs Hotel burned in 1930, and the site gradually returned to its natural state.

Sometime about 1900, the River Road was straightened and relocated from the east side of the Carson House to the west side. A new porch was added to the west side of the house so the west side became the front, and the family cemetery is now in front of the house instead of in the rear. The River Road is now called the John B. Gordon Road.

The Carson Family Cemetery at the Carson Place, where four Confederate veterans, their parents, several of their children and grandchildren and two of their wives and several other descendants lie buried, is now maintained by a trust.

Joe, Jr. was "stricken with paralysis" at the courthouse on February 28, 1889, and passed away on March 25 at his home in Reynolds. "He was a gallant soldier, a model officer, and everywhere and at all times a modest gentleman and a consistent Christian." After his death, Charlotte Briggs Carson moved to Tifton, Georgia, to live with her son, Briggs.

Saphronia died in 1886 at age 72 at the home of her daughter, Martha, in Columbus, Georgia.

Melissa moved in with her sister-in-law Annie Elizabeth in 1900, and in 1910, Melissa moved to Kissimmee, Florida, to live with her son Charles A. "Charlie" Carson, a banker. Melissa passed away in 1912.

Over the 150 years after the war, the Carson family dispersed themselves all over the United States, and now there are no family members remaining in Macon County, Georgia. However, there are still several black people named Carson in the area.

Jefferson Davis was arrested for treason but never tried, and freed two years later. In his later years he became an advocate for reconciliation with the Union.

Confederate General John B. Gordon became a strong opponent of reconstruction. He went on to become both a United States Senator and the Governor of Georgia. Incidentally, Gordon bought a vacation home called Beechwood Plantation just up the road from the Carson Place in 1888, where he raised cattle and other crops.

Confederate General Robert E. Lee became president of Washington College after the war. Upon his death in 1870, the college was renamed "Washington and Lee University."

Atlanta became Georgia's state capitol in 1868, replacing Milledgeville.

The last Federal occupation troops left Georgia during General Grant's presidency in 1871.

Cotton may still be king of Georgia agriculture, but other crops such as cattle, soy beans, peanuts, pine trees for wood pulp, and even sod for landscaping now occupy much of the land that was once devoted to cotton.

Slavery is gone, and the New South has risen in its place. Old times may be gone, but "old times there are not forgotten. Look away, look away, look away, Dixie Land!"

There was a South of slavery and secession - that South is dead. There is now a South of union and freedom - that South, thank God, is living, breathing, and growing every hour.

Atlanta newspaper editor Henry W. Grady
In a speech in New York
1886

Bibliography

Adams, John R. Sr. "The Carson Family," *Taylor County Tracer*, Taylor County Historical-Genealogical Association, Inc., Butler, Georgia, July, 2000.

"Battle of Antietam." last modified September 19, 2015, https://en.wikipedia.org/wiki/Battle_of_Antietam.

"Battle of Cedar Mountain." October 10, 2015, https://en.wikipedia.org/wiki/Battle_of_Cedar_Mountain.

"Battle of Cheat Mountain." last modified December 13, 2014, https://en.wikipedia.org/wiki/Battle_of_Cheat_Mountain.

"Battle of Fort Stedman." last modified October 13, 2015, https://en.wikipedia.org/wiki/Battle_of_Fort_Stedman.

"Battle of Front Royal." last modified November 4, 2015, https://en.wikipedia.org/wiki/Battle_of_Front_Royal.

"Battle of Gettysburg." last modified November 20, 2015, https://en.wikipedia.org/wiki/Battle_of_Gettysburg.

"Battle of McDowell." last modified June 29, 2015, https://en.wikipedia.org/wiki/Battle_of_McDowell.

"Battle of Monocacy." last modified November 10, 2015, https://en.wikipedia.org/wiki/Battle_of_Monocacy.

"Battle of Spotsylvania Courthouse." last modified November 16, 2015, https://en.wikipedia.org/wiki/Battle_of_Spotsylvania_Court_House.

"Benjamin Hawkins." last modified November 17, 2015, https://en.wikipedia.org/wiki/Benjamin_Hawkins.

"Burning the Wrightsville Bridge." http://www.pacivilwartrails.com/stories/tales/burning-the-wrightsville-bridge.

"Civil War Salt Lists." 2014, http://www.genealogytoday.com/guide/civil-war-salt-lists.html.

"Confederate Hospitals in Lynchburg." 2011, http://www.gravegarden.org/confederate-hospitals-in-lynchburg/

"Confederate Railroads in the American Civil War." last modified November 2, 2015, https://en.wikipedia.org/wiki/Confederate_railroads_in_the_American_Civil_War.

"Crawford County, Georgia." last modified August 29, 2015, https://en.wikipedia.org/wiki/Crawford_County,_Georgia.

"Economy of the Confederate States of America." last modified November 7, 2015, https://en.wikipedia.org/wiki/Economy_of_the_Confederate_States_of_America.

"Fall of Richmond." http://www.civilwaracademy.com/fall-of-richmond.html.

"First Battle of Winchester." last modified March 26, 2015, https://en.wikipedia.org/wiki/First_Battle_of_Winchester.

"Flags of the Confederate States of America." last modified November 16, 2015, https://en.wikipedia.org/wiki/Flags_of_the_Confederate_States_of_America.

"Foods of the American Civil War." last modified October 1, 2015, https://en.wikipedia.org/wiki/Foods_of_the_American_Civil_War.

"Foot Cavalry." last modified September 15, 2014, https://en.wikipedia.org/wiki/Foot_cavalry.

"Fort Delaware." last modified on August 15, 2015, https://en.wikipedia.org/wiki/Fort_Delaware.

Fowler, Ryland Dean (Ed.). *Macon County Life 1933-1983*. Macon County (Georgia) Historical Society, 1983.

Gordon, John B. *Reminiscences of the Civil War*. Atlanta: Charles Scribner's Sons, 1903.

"Gordonsville, Virginia." last modified August 31, 2015, https://en.wikipedia.org/wiki/Gordonsville,_Virginia.

Gorman, M. D. "General Hospital #9." last modified July 17, 2008, http://www.mdgorman.com/Hospitals/general_hospital_9.htm.

Gorman, M. D. " Jackson Hospital." last modified May 2, 2008, http://www.mdgorman.com/Hospitals/jackson_hospital.htm.

Gorman, M. D. " Stuart Hospital." last modified February 12, 2008, http://www.mdgorman.com/Hospitals/stuart_hospital.htm.

"Greencastle, Pennsylvania." last modified November 7, 2015, https://en.wikipedia.org/wiki/Greencastle,_Pennsylvania.

"Hardtack." last modified November 15, 2015, https://en.wikipedia.org/wiki/Hardtack.

Harp, Emily H., and Forsling, Elizabeth H. *History of the First Baptist Church Reynolds, Georgia, 1832-1982.*

Hays, Mrs. J. E, "Brief History of Macon County," *The Butler Herald*, Butler, Georgia, July 2, 1936.

Hays, Louise Frederick. *History of Macon County Georgia.* The County Commissioners, Atlanta, Georgia: Stein Printing Company, 1933.

Henderson, Lillian. *Roster of the Confederate Soldiers of Georgia 1861-1865.* Hapeville, Georgia: Longino and Porter, Inc.

Howard, Tina Clark, contributor. "Elim Baptist Church Proceedings Crawford County Georgia 1828-1866." http://files.usgwarchives.net/ga/crawford/churches/elim.txt.

"Immortal Six Hundred." last modified June 26, 2015, https://en.wikipedia.org/wiki/Immortal_Six_Hundred.

"James Osgood Andrew." last modified May 1, 2015, https://en.wikipedia.org/wiki/James_Osgood_Andrew.

"Jefferson Davis." last modified November 18, 2015, https://en.wikipedia.org/wiki/Jefferson_Davis.

"John Brown Gordon." last modified September 22, 2015, https://en.wikipedia.org/wiki/John_Brown_Gordon.

Lechner, James. "The Carson Family of Georgia." *Taylor County Tracer*, Taylor County Historical-Genealogical Association, Inc., Butler, Georgia, August, 2000.

"Macon County Volunteers." *Journal & Messenger*, Macon, Georgia, May 8, 1861.

"Meeting in Macon County." *Journal & Messenger*, Macon, Georgia, November 27, 1860.

"Mercer University." last modified November 18, 2015, https://en.wikipedia.org/wiki/Mercer_University.

"Milledgeville." 2015, http://www.georgiaencyclopedia.org/articles/counties-cities-neighborhoods/milledgeville.

Moore, Violet. "Pleasant Grove Baptist Church Over 100 Years Old," *Citizen and Georgian,* Montezuma, Georgia, December 15, 1976.

Moore, Violet. "The Old Farms: What They Are Today," *The Atlanta Journal*, October 30, 1974.

"Penfield, Georgia." last modified on November 6, 2014, https://en.wikipedia.org/wiki/Penfield,_Georgia.

"Reconstruction in Georgia." 2015, http://www.georgiaencyclopedia.org/articles/history-archaeology/reconstruction-georgia.

"Richard B. Garnett." last modified on July 10, 2015, https://en.wikipedia.org/wiki/Richard_B._Garnett.

"Richmond in the American Civil War." last modified on October 26, 2015, https://en.wikipedia.org/wiki/Richmond_in_the_American_Civil_War.

"Robert H. Milroy." last modified on August 4, 2015, https://en.wikipedia.org/wiki/Robert_H._Milroy.

"Secession." 2015, http://www.georgiaencyclopedia.org/articles/history-archaeology/secession.

"Sharecropping." 2015, http://www.georgiaencyclopedia.org/articles/history-archaeology/sharecropping.

"Staunton and Parkersburg Turnpike." last modified October 4, 2014, https://en.wikipedia.org/wiki/Staunton_and_Parkersburg_Turnpike.

"Stonewall Jackson." last modified November 21, 2015, https://en.wikipedia.org/wiki/Stonewall_Jackson.

Taylor County Turns Back the Clock. Butler, Georgia: The Taylor County News and Butler Herald, 1976 (?).

Thomas, Henry W. *History of the Doles-Cook Brigade, Army of Northern Virginia, C. S. A.* Morningside, 1988.

"Tribute to Captain J. P. Carson, Late of Reynolds, Early History of Taylor County Reviewed from Files of the Herald." *The Butler Herald*, Butler, Georgia, September 9, 1937.

"United States Presidential Election, 1860." last modified on November 19, 2015, https://en.wikipedia.org/wiki/United_States_presidential_election,_1860.

"Whitworth Rifle." last modified on September 3, 2015, https://en.wikipedia.org/wiki/Whitworth_rifle.

"William Ward (Texas)." last modified on January 9, 2015, https://en.wikipedia.org/wiki/William_Ward_(Texas).

"Wilson's Raid." last modified on September 21, 2015, https://en.wikipedia.org/wiki/Wilson%27s_Raid.

Wilson, W. T.. Lt. 4th Ga. Regt., letter to *The Butler Herald*, Butler, Georgia, September 23, 1879.

"Winchester, Virginia, in the American Civil War." last modified on February 16, 2015, https://en.wikipedia.org/wiki/Winchester,_Virginia_in_the_American_Civil_War.

Young, J. R. "Slavery in Antebellum Georgia." last updated September 28, 2015, http://www.georgiaencyclopedia.org/articles/history-archaeology/slavery-antebellum-georgia.

"Zouave." Wikipedia, November 16, 2015, https://en.wikipedia.org/wiki/Zouave.

Printed in the United States
By Bookmasters